DARTMOUᴿ

DARTMOOR

INTO THE WILDERNESS

MICHELLE DIBB

'Tree at Bonehill.' (Mike Bartholomew)

Front cover image: 'Into the Wilderness.' (Mike Bartholomew)

Back cover image: 'Stormy Clouds at Belstone.' (Mike Bartholomew)

First published 2011

The History Press
The Mill, Brimscombe Port
Stroud, Gloucestershire, GL5 2QG
www.thehistorypress.co.uk

British Library Cataloguing in Publication Data.
A catalogue record for this book is available from the British Library.

ISBN 978 0 7524 5929 5

Typesetting and origination by The History Press
Printed in Great Britain

CONTENTS

'Where the Ponies Run Free.' (Miles Wolstenholme)

Step outside and taste the air after rain,
Try to see beyond the city smoke,

See the colours as they really are,
Listen to the river, the breeze caught in the trees.

Feel the weather on your skin,
Stand small amidst mountains.

Watch flowers and grasses tremble and sway,
Observe through warm eyes.

Tread carefully, guardian of creation,
We were only given one world.

Scott Morrish

ACKNOWLEDGEMENTS

The stunning photography in this book was kindly contributed by Mike Bartholomew and Miles Wolstenholme. Thank you both. Thanks also to Mike Nendick at Dartmoor National Park Authority; Tim Sandles at www.legendarydartmoor.co.uk; Brian Dingle, HM Prison Service, Princetown; and the poets who kindly contributed their beautiful poems: Scott Morrish, www.glebecottagestudio.co.uk; Fenella Montgomery, www.moorpoets.org.uk; and Jennie Osborne, www.moorpoets.org.uk. A big thank you also to Louise Webb and Pam Fey for providing the illustrations.

For Koah and Mum, I love you both

INTRODUCTION

There is no true wilderness left in England any more. Man has left his footprint in most of our soils as he has settled and toiled over the centuries. Now most of England is covered by cities, houses, roads or farm land – and even the stars are dulled by our lights.

A few places are left, however, where the formidable environment has prevented man from leaving such a significant imprint. Dartmoor is one of those places; a wilderness untamed, harsh but beautiful, and steeped in mystery and history.

We can stand in the middle of Dartmoor and view the horizon under a wide expanse of sky. We can breathe pure, unpolluted air, smell the wild heather and gorse, listen to streams trickling and skylarks calling. We can find solitude and peace away from our busy lives. Immersing our senses in nature, we can feel a sense of our own wildness, a sense of where we truly belong.

Scattered over the moor you will find evidence of man's existence here since prehistoric times. The remains of these ancient relics only hint at how we once lived, the rest is a mystery.

'Belstone Common.' (Mike Bartholomew)

one

HOW DARTMOOR WAS FORMED

Dartmoor was formed around 280 million years ago, when the earth's plates moved, causing the sedimentary rocks to heat up and turn into magma (hot molten rock). The magma was forced upwards and, before it reached the earth's surface, it crystallised into a massive layer of granite (a plutonic or intrusive rock). Over millions of years, the earth and rocks above were weathered away to expose the granite.

Geologists believe there is a huge granite mass under the ground running between the Scilly Isles and Dartmoor. Dartmoor itself is a granite area of 241 square miles (625 square km) and is one of six granite regions in the West of England which are the extruding parts of the granite mass.

SHAPING THE LANDSCAPE

The word granite comes from the Latin *granum*, meaning grain. When the granite mass was cooling and solidifying from the molten rock all those millions of years ago, the minerals crystallised into closely interlocking grains to form the hard rock. If you look very closely at a lump of granite, you will see the three main minerals that make it up:

- Quartz – the translucent grey-looking grains
- Feldspar – the white grains, sometimes stained yellow or pink and sometimes forming large white crystals
- Biotite – the dark brown glistening flakes

THE FORMING OF TIN, COPPER AND OTHER MINERALS

The granite first turned solid and then slowly cooled. As it did, the contraction caused vertical joints, known as open fractures, to form. Movement of the granite caused the fractures to become faults. At the same time, large quantities of hot, salty water were released by the cooling of the granite and this moved upwards through the joints into the cooler top of the granite, carrying dissolved minerals such as quartz, tin and tourmaline. As the temperature fell, the dissolved minerals crystallised into veins of tin, copper, iron and arsenic, which miners call lodes.

Between 65 million and 145 million years ago, the sea level rose and Dartmoor was under water. Sea creatures lived and died here, turning to chalk and dropping to the bottom of the ocean to form a thin layer of chalk over the granite.

'Shelstone Tor.' (Miles Wolstenholme)

'Rocks on Yar Tor.' (Miles Wolstenholme)

The uncovering of the granite

As the sea level dropped the granite mass was revealed, covered with a layer of chalk, slate and sandstone around 2–3km thick. This was worn away over the next 10 million years, resulting in the rich red soils around Exeter, Crediton and East Devon. Fragments of granite can be found amongst the red sandstone rocks. As the pressure on the granite decreased the rock expanded, and this caused the horizontal joints to form.

Kaolinisation

The next stage of the process was kaolinisation: the circulation of heated water through the joints caused the feldspar minerals to decompose, making white clay, or kaolin. It is predominant around Lee Moor and mining of the clay has been happening for years. This process probably occurred over a long period of time, and started to shape the tors as the granite around them was softened and weakened in places.

Chemical weathering

Around 60 million years ago, the climate was hot and wet and Dartmoor was covered by a sub-tropical forest which included the Giant Redwood tree (sequoia) and also palms, ferns and heathers. The acidic waters seeped deep into the granite, penetrating the existing joints and causing the granite to break apart. This process is called chemical weathering.

The Ice Ages

Between 2 million and 11,000 years ago, it is thought that we went through about twenty ice ages with temperatures as low as -20°C. Dartmoor was covered in snow and frozen solid. Ice crystals swelled in the rock crevices and the pressure caused rock fragments to break off, littering the slopes with debris. The freezing and thawing conditions forced the deeply-weathered granite to break up into boulders and rocks. Beneath the soil was a frozen layer and, during the summer, the surface layer of this would melt, causing the boulders, rocks and soil to move down the slope, leaving the tors, which hadn't been so weathered, standing tall. The scattered boulders you see around some of the tors, known as clitter, are the remains of this movement, as are the long lines of large boulders called boulder runs, and the gravelly material which surrounds the tors, known as growan.

During the warm periods, the land was covered by tundra vegetation of small flowering plants and shrubs, and only small trees such as dwarf willows grew here.

There is a quarry at Higher Cherrybrook Bridge, in between Postbridge and Two Bridges, where you can see examples of each of the stages of the process. It has been designated by English Nature as a Regionally Important Geological Site (RIGS). These are sites which show a range of geological features and are selected for their scientific, educational, historical and aesthetic value.

The tors

The Oxford English Dictionary describes a tor as:

> A hill or rocky peak, esp. in Devon or Cornwall. From the Old English word 'torr' Gaelic 'torr' 'bulging hill'.

It has been suggested that there are 147 tors on Dartmoor, but the ambiguous classification of what a tor actually is makes it difficult to assess how many tors there are. There are the obvious granite outcrops, but there are also hills with a few boulders on top which might be considered tors.

'Sharp Tor and Hare Tor.' (Miles Wolstenholme)

ROCK BASINS

A rock basin is a smooth bowl-like depression which can occur on the top of a rock. Some believe they are naturally occurring, whilst others believe they were made by the Druids. The scientific explanation is that they are a product of localised weathering and are formed when weak feldspar crystals are split by the frost, loosened, and then eventually blown away by the wind. Over time, a hollow starts to form and fills with rainwater. In the winter the water freezes and, upon thawing, more fragments are eroded which are again blown away by the wind.

The mystical theory, which came about during the 1800s, was that the Druids carved the basins to use in their rituals and ceremonies, or to use as cisterns to collect pure rain water which would then be used in their ceremonies.

Other examples of rock basins can be found on: Kes Tor, Hel Tor, Pew Tor, Gutter Tor, Mel Tor, Bag Tor, and Great Mis Tor (supposedly formed by the Devil himself for use in his evil rites).

LOGAN STONES

Logan stones are natural rock formations where a top slab of granite appears to rest on a pivot on top of a tor or clump of rocks. They are formed as a horizontal joint in the granite is eroded and enough weathering has taken place to separate the top slab from its base. The stone rests on a pivot and can be rocked or 'logged' without it over-balancing.

Over the years, many of the logan stones have stopped rocking. In a couple of cases this is due to vandalism. The army have tried to restore a couple of the stones but it seems impossible to make them rock again.

Other logan stones are: the Hanging Stone at Hangingstone Hill; the Rugglestone at Widecombe; the Nutcrackers at Lustleigh Cleave; and Nutcracker Rock at Rippon Tor. There are also various smaller logan stones which you might step on by mistake at the top of a tor – you'll know when you feel yourself move.

THE RIVERS

Dartmoor rivers are amazingly diverse and extremely beautiful. Sprouting out of the ground as a boggy spring on the peat-layered upper moor, the beginnings of a Dartmoor river grow into a small, clear gravel-bed stream, gurgling through the grassy moorland over rocks and boulders, then become a rushing, tumbling torrent with cascading waterfalls, flowing over the edge of the granite mass to finally settle as a meandering river, leaving Dartmoor and heading for the sea.

The river pattern on Dartmoor is a world-famous example of a radial drainage pattern (radiating outwards), with the initial location of the rivers being established all those millions of years ago when the granite was first uncovered.

During the ice ages when the snow melted, the floods, ice jams and rock flows eroded the land away to form the valley floors. During the warmer periods, fine sand and gravel were deposited, forming the river terraces – one of the main sources of tin. At the edges of the moors, the steep valley slopes caused many gorges and waterfalls to be formed.

The rivers arising on Dartmoor include the East and West Okement, the Taw, the Teign, the Bovey, the Dart, the Avon, the Yealm, the Erme, the Plym, the Walkham, the Tavy and the Lyd. Dartmoor rivers are known as 'torrent rivers' as they are fast rising when it rains and quick to fall again when it stops. Due to this phenomenon, not much plant life grows in the water itself, and it looks clean and pure as it passes over its gravel bed. The banks, however, are abundant with rich mosses and ferns such as the royal fern, the lemon-scented or mountain fern, and filmy ferns.

Salmon and trout are the main fish found in Dartmoor rivers, and the main birds you will spot perched on boulders are grey wagtails (*see* p.142) and dippers (*see* p.154).

'East Okement River.' (Miles Wolstenholme)

ANCIENT WOODLANDS

At the end of the last ice age, around 11,500 years ago, the climate on Dartmoor warmed and, over the next 5,000 years, the vegetation changed slowly from a tundra vegetation to a more European temperate forest. The land mass of Great Britain was still connected to Europe at this time, and seeds slowly drifted over to take root on Dartmoor. Oak, birch, hazel and elm started to grow and Dartmoor became covered in forests, predominantly oak. If it wasn't for the presence of man, it would still be wooded.

Today, however, only a few areas of ancient woodland are left. These are generally along steep river valleys and in areas inaccessible to man. Wistman's Wood (*see* p.138), Black a Tor Copse (*see* p.110), Hembury Woods, Holne Woods, the Teign Valley Woods and Lower Dart Valley are some of the remains of Dartmoor's ancient woodland, along with some of the woodlands along parish boundaries.

The Dartmoor National Park Authority is assisting owners of ancient woodland areas in restoring and enhancing them, as woodland is one of Dartmoor's richest and most important habitats. Many woodland areas have been neglected, or have been planted with non-native species in the past.

PEAT

When man first arrived on Dartmoor in around 10000 BC, conditions were wetter. People cleared the forests from the high ground in order to attract animals to graze in the clearings, thereby making hunting a lot easier. Along with natural forest fires, this left the bare soil vulnerable to the wet conditions, and the decomposition of vegetation on the growan or clay subsoil caused peat bogs to form. The peat soaked up the water like a sponge and was therefore infertile, which meant the forests couldn't regrow. Eventually these bogs spread, and in this way most of the high ground of Dartmoor lost its wooded cover.

Over a third of the open moor is covered with peat, which is around 50cm thick; in some places it is 7m deep. Peat is no longer accumulating and is thought to have been formed under wetter conditions than we have today. In geological terms, peat is important as it contains preserved pollen which can tell us a lot about the environment and vegetation of Dartmoor since the last ice age.

two

THE ARRIVAL OF MAN

Humans have been on Dartmoor since the Stone Age. At first just nomadic, impermanent hunter-gatherers searching for food, then settling and establishing homesteads. The moors would have been much warmer, with lush wooded lands providing food and plenty of springs and streams for water; a perfect place to settle and start to grow crops and domesticate animals.

The Stone Age consists of three periods in time:

- Palaeolithic (from 2.5 million years ago – 10000 BC)
- Mesolithic or Middle Stone Age (10000 BC – 4500 BC)
- Neolithic or New Stone Age (4500 BC – 2300 BC)

MIDDLE STONE AGE

By 10000 BC, most of the moor was covered in thick woodland, as was most of Britain. It was the end of the last ice age and the climate was warming up. This is the period known as the Mesolithic or Middle Stone Age. Man was a hunter-gatherer and tribes moved over the moors in search of food. They began to clear the forests in order to create grazing land for the wild animals, probably near sources of drinking water. The cleared areas attracted the animals, which were then easy prey for the hunters, who probably also managed their quarry to make sure the herds of deer and other prey were not depleted. No evidence of any kind of permanent dwelling from that time period exists, suggesting that the population was nomadic and existed on nuts, berries, leaves, fruits and roots, as well as the hunted meat.

NEOLITHIC OR NEW STONE AGE

The shift from a hunter-gatherer way of life to farming is what defines the transition from Middle to New Stone Age. During the Neolithic (New Stone Age) period, people appeared to be more settled. More of the forests were cleared and farms were established in the lowlands. Crops and animals were beginning to be domesticated. Seeds brought over from Europe were grown and this is what probably caused man to settle. The only evidence of life from this period found on Dartmoor are some flint tools and flint shavings, a handful of earth burial mounds (long mounds) and some stone chambers from around 3000 BC.

END OF THE NEOLITHIC PERIOD TO THE BEGINNING OF THE BRONZE AGE

During the end of the Neolithic Period, as well as the first large communal tombs, known as chamber tombs, some of the earliest ceremonial monuments were constructed. Their exact purpose is not known but it is thought that people from communities in a particular region would gather together, probably at regular intervals, for ritual practices, to socialise, to meet new partners, or to acquire fresh livestock and to exchange ceremonial gifts.

Some of the great ceremonial monuments of this time in the UK were aligned according to the position of the sun during the winter or summer solstice. These are known as causewayed enclosures. The long opening of a passage grave would be positioned to allow the sun – on the shortest few days of the year – to shine directly into the central burial chamber. The so-called 'henge' monuments, like Stonehenge, seem to have developed out of the causewayed enclosures from around 3000 BC. They also incorporate lunar and solar alignments, which are seen as a means of uniting the physical and social structures of human societies with the powers of the natural world.

Most of the ancient monuments and remains of prehistoric dwellings on Dartmoor are from the end of the New Stone Age and the beginning of the Bronze Age. Many of the stone rows and circles were built during this time and, although their specific purpose isn't known, it is believed that they were for religious or ceremonial purposes.

STONE ROWS

A stone row on Dartmoor can be anything from 32m to 3.4km long (the world's largest) and from 2.5m to less than 10cm high. There are more than seventy stone rows on Dartmoor, with nearly half of them being single rows. Almost the same number are formed of parallel lines and are called double stone rows. There are five known examples of triple or multiple stone rows.

'Merrivale Stone Rows.' (Miles Wolstenholme)

'Shoveldown Stone Rows.' (Miles Wolstenholme)

Almost three quarters of the Dartmoor stone rows have a burial monument at one end, similar to the causewayed enclosures described above, and a number of them have a tall terminal stone (or menhir) at one end. Some stone rows terminate in a blocking stone – a stone set sideways across the end of a row.

MENHIRS

Menhirs are tall, upright stones (the tallest being the Drizzlecombe Bone at 4.2m (*see* p.83). They are thought to be part of a ceremonial site that contains stone rows and stone circles, although some are found standing alone. Being visible from afar, they may have had both a practical and a symbolic role, either as territorial markers, way markers or perhaps meeting points.

STONE CIRCLES

The stone circles are largish circles of upright stones, with their flat faces pointing into the circle. As there is no evidence that these were connected to burials, they are thought to have been used for ritual purposes. Many of them were re-erected during the nineteenth century, and at the same time large amounts of charcoal were discovered, suggesting that fire played a part in whatever activity took place within these monuments.

The location of the circles is significant in that many of them have commanding views to distant horizons or are situated on watersheds, suggesting that they have strong links with their surrounding landscapes and were significant points on lines of communication. They have also been the subject of a great deal of astronomical analysis, but nothing has been proven. It is thought that they also incorporate lunar and solar alignments, which are believed to provide unifying effects between nature and man. This is a subject of much debate.

'Beardown Man, Beardown Hill.' (Mike Bartholomew)

CHAMBER TOMBS OR LONG BARROWS

The move into the Bronze Age period didn't bring huge changes, but the way people were buried changed from the use of one long barrow or chamber tomb to small, individual graves.

In the Neolithic era, chamber tombs or barrows were often used over a period of time for multiple burials of the same social or family group, and in some cases they appear to have been used for individuals of a higher status. They were long earthen mounds with a stone chamber at one end. There are two types of chamber tomb which have been found on Dartmoor, one made of earth and the other made with large stones; these are known as megalithic or long barrows. Spinsters Rock (*see* p.125) is the remains of a chamber tomb. There is also one on Butterdon Hill and two on the slope of Buttern Hill, near Gidleigh.

CISTS, KISTS OR KISTVAENS

Cists or kists, small stone-built coffins sunk into the ground, started to replace the chamber tomb. Kistvaen is the local name for a cist and comes from the word 'cist-veyn', meaning a stone chest. The body was placed in the kistvaen in a crouched position, and when cremation was carried out the ashes were placed inside a crude pottery urn. What is notable about Dartmoor kistvaens is that they are always oriented in a NW/SE direction. Once again, it is thought that this was so the deceased was facing the sun.

Most of the kistvaens were excavated in the nineteenth or early twentieth century, and shards of beaker-shaped pots, flint arrowheads and other artefacts were found.

CAIRNS

Once people were being buried individually, the use of cairns became widespread. There are 1,310 round cairns and over 210 ring cairns on Dartmoor, so you will probably see at least one during your visit, even if you don't know it's a prehistoric cairn. Merrivale and Drizzlecombe are good areas to visit if you wish to see examples of cairns.

'The Merrivale Kistvaen.' (Miles Wolstenholme)

Round Cairns

Round cairns (a man-made pile of stones, often erected over a cist as the landmark to a burial site) succeeded the chamber tombs and, although some may have covered more than one individual interment, the smaller ones did not. Cairns varied in size from 3–4m in diameter, and less than 1m in height, to well over 20m and sometimes as much as 40m in diameter and 3.5m in height. The smaller cairns are believed to be generally earlier in date; the larger cairns sited on hill tops were probably also territory markers.

In some areas, a few groups of between twenty and thirty small cairns have been found. The cairns are very low and often only distinguishable because they are covered with different vegetation to the surrounding area.

Cairn Circles

Cairn circles are single burials covered by a low round cairn. The limits of the cairn are marked by a circle of upright granite slabs, not touching each other, often leaning outwards.

Kerb Circle

A kerb circle is a single burial (often within a cist) which was covered by a shallow spread of stone. The monument was then bounded by a close-set ring of low stones.

Ring Cairns

A ring cairn is a level or slightly hollowed area surrounded by a low circular or oval stone bank. Two examples on Dartmoor were excavated and the pits were found to contain charcoal, but no evidence of a burial was discovered, although similar monuments in Wales contain burials. Dartmoor ring cairns are thought to have been constructed around 1800–1600 BC.

Tor Cairns

A tor cairn is where one of the tors is surrounded by a low bank of stone, or enclosed in a cairn.

FARMING AND SETTLEMENTS

The reason there is such an abundance of Neolithic and Bronze Age remains on Dartmoor is because the remnants are granite, which isn't easily eroded. Hardly any pottery, bone or metal from prehistoric times has survived, as the soil acidity on Dartmoor is high.

By the middle of the Bronze Age, most of the trees had been cleared from high Dartmoor and man began creating fields in which to grow their crops and graze their animals. The fields were long strips of land, with low stony banks called reaves built to separate them. Reaves were also built to mark land boundaries.

Four main types of reave have been identified. Terminal Reaves are boundaries which cut across the slopes of Dartmoor, defining the limits of enclosed land. Parallel Reaves are where the land within these boundaries was further divided by the construction of parallel land boundaries set at right angles to the terminal reave, up and down the hill and valley slopes. These created the long, narrow, rectangular fields. Cross Reaves created even smaller fields within the parallel reaves. Contour Reaves snaked across the contours of the slopes, particularly on the southern and western sides of Dartmoor, above the main areas of prehistoric enclosures. They are thought to mark a division between grazing zones.

THE FIRST PERMANENT DWELLINGS

Inside some of the fields, the remains of 'hut circles' or 'roundhouses' have been found, which suggests that shepherds would stay here temporarily during the summer months when they brought their cattle up to graze. Hut circles can also be found away from the field systems, usually grouped together and surrounded by a stone wall (a pound). A wonderful example of a pound is Grimspound, which has around twenty-four hut circles enclosed within its wall. Here they could grow crops and bring their cattle in at night for protection (see p.149).

There are over 5,000 Bronze Age roundhouses or hut circles. They are usually circular and range in size from 6ft (1.8m) to 30ft (9m) in diameter. All that remains of them now are the outer granite walls. These walls would have been a double circle of wall, about 3-4ft high, made out of granite boulders. There would have been a ring of posts standing upright in the wall which would have supported the roof timbers (branches). A tall post would have stood in the centre, where the roof timbers met. The roof was then covered with turf, gorse or heather. Some hut circles had porches and some circles were joined together to form two rooms.

Beds were usually a low stone platform covered with animal skins and heather, often located by the side of the door. For cooking there would have been a hearth on which to burn a fire, with a hole in the roof through which the smoke escaped. Next to the hearth you would find a shallow hole for cooking. Stones would be heated in the fire and dropped into the water in order to cook.

THE IRON AGE

Roundhouses were built and lived in until into the Iron Age. There are few Iron Age remains on the high moor; it appears that the climate was changing at the end of the Bronze Age and people started to move away from the centre of the moor to the more sheltered surrounding lowlands. It is also thought that the soil would have become infertile and acidic due to over farming, and this would have led to crop failures and food shortage on the high moor.

During this time, defended settlements (hill forts) were built to protect people, their houses, the outbuildings and the animals from their neighbours. There are around a dozen hill forts on Dartmoor, all found on top of hills of course. Deep ditches were dug and high banks built to protect the community from possible attack. It appears that life was getting more aggressive.

'Hut Circle at Merrivale.' (Miles Wolstenholme)

The best-known examples of Iron Age hill forts are Prestonbury Castle near Drewsteignton (*see* p.126), Cranbrook Castle near Moretonhampstead and Hembury Castle near Buckfastleigh.

SCHEDULED ANCIENT MONUMENTS

Over 1,200 of Dartmoor's prehistoric sites are classified as Scheduled Ancient Monuments. This means the site is considered to be of national importance by the government and is given legal protection against unauthorised change. A schedule has been kept since 1882 in the UK and there are currently 19,717 entries and 31,400 sites. The current legislation, the Ancient Monuments and Archaeological Areas Act 1979, specifies a formal system of Scheduled Monument Consent for any work to a designated monument.

THE ANGLO-SAXONS

Anglo-Saxon settlers arrived in England around AD 450, invading from across the North Sea and settling. They gradually moved to the West Country and reached Devon in about AD 700, clearing the land and burning and cutting down the forests to make large communal fields. These large open fields were divided into strips and allocated to individual families. The farmers started to share resources, sharing ploughs and agreeing on which crops each would grow, exchanging strips of land and hedging their fields. Animals were still taken onto the moors to graze during the summers.

There are no physical above-ground remains of Anglo-Saxon houses to be found on Dartmoor, nor in fact anywhere in England. The houses were simple dwellings, constructed using timber and thatch, and sometimes the foundations were of stone. Evidence of Anglo-Saxon remains has been discovered on the sites of some of the existing Dartmoor churches. Buckfastleigh church is one example of this (*see* p.72).

At this time, the whole of Devon was a 'forest' and was the Crown's hunting ground. It was mainly wooded and many animals lived here, protected by strict laws. Lydford was an Anglo-Saxon defensive site established as one of the four Saxon burhs (*see* p.106) by King Alfred the Great, one of the kings of Wessex. The Forest of Dartmoor then became the hunting ground of the Wessex kings and the land was no longer free for people to access. It became known as the Royal Forest.

It was the Saxons who divided Dartmoor into individual lands, which set the boundaries for today's parishes; each area was owned by a Saxon thane.

THE NORMANS

When the Normans arrived in 1066 things began to change and, over the years, the manorial system was introduced. This meant that each area, now called a 'manor', had a Lord of the Manor who held all the legal and economic power. He was supported economically from his own land-holding and also from obligatory contributions (taxes) from the peasant population (serfs) under his jurisdiction. Many of the parish boundaries today on Dartmoor are the original manors. The 'Forest of Dartmoor' referred to the highland in the centre of the moor. The manor's boundaries were created so that each manor would touch the boundary of the forest – so the people of the manors could reach the forest without having to cross into another manor.

There was much unrest amongst the people of Devon about the strict forest laws that were imposed. The people forced a charter from King John, for which he was paid, declaring that Devon was to be disafforested with the exception of Dartmoor and Exmoor. Later, when Henry III was reigning, he gave the Forest of Dartmoor, along with the manor of Lydford and Lydford Castle, to his brother Richard III and that is how it passed to the Duchy of Cornwall. It then became a 'chase', which it still is.

From the thirteenth century, the villagers of the twenty-four manors surrounding the forest were granted 'venville' rights in exchange for paying rents to the Duchy of Cornwall. The word venville is derived from the Latin *fines villarum*, meaning 'a variable sum to be paid by members of a settlement for use of common resources'.

The forest was then divided into four quarters and each quarter had an 'agister', or moorman, to look after the grazing and welfare of cattle on his quarter. The venville tenants were allowed to graze their cattle on the moor (the forest) but had to bring them off at the end of the day. If their cattle was found on the forest at night it would be driven to a pound and a fine would have to be paid to get them back. As well as paying rent to the agisters, they would also have to attend the annual drifts.

THE ANNUAL DRIFTS

The drifts happened once a year, usually during the summer. There was a drift for ponies (*see* p.37) and a separate drift for the cattle. All the cattle and ponies of the forest were rounded up and driven to the pound for that quarter. Here, a Duchy Official would oversee proceedings and the farmers would claim their animals back. The animals belonging to venville farmers were allowed to go free but all other owners had to pay a fine. Any animals that weren't claimed were kept for a maximum of twenty-one days and were then considered to be the property of the Duchy, and were consequently sold at Princetown Fair.

The people who lived in 'ancient tenements', of which Prince Hall is an example (*see* p.137), were free holders. They had the right to enclose land, take turf and peat from the forest and graze their livestock there. In return, they carried out administrative duties.

'Hound Tor Medieval Settlement.' (Miles Wolstenholme)

COMMONERS' RIGHTS

Those who lived within the Forest of Dartmoor held commoners' rights unconditionally and did not have to pay rent. This meant they had access to everything except vert (green oak) and venison. Over the centuries, the rights have come to include:

- depasturage – the right to graze sheep, cattle, and ponies
- turbary – the right to take turf for fuel for domestic use
- estovers – the right to take underwood or branches for fuel or repairs
- piscary – the right to take fish
- pannage – the right to allow pigs to eat acorns and beech mast
- swaling – the right to burn heather, grass and gorse, and the right to take sand, gravel or stone for use on their holding

Over the years, disputes over rights have occurred. The Commons Registration Act of 1965 required the registration of common land nationally, its ownership, and the extent and nature of the rights held. On Dartmoor today there are ninety-two separate common land units coming under some fifty-four different owners, and there are about 850 registered commoners.

The commons of Dartmoor are the areas of open pasturage which lie between the forest and the manor boundaries to which they are connected. About two fifths of Dartmoor is common land today.

MEDIEVAL DWELLINGS

In medieval times, the field systems were connected; the boundaries were marked by a corn ditch (a stone wall with a ditch facing out onto the open moor and a sloping bank on the farmland side). This prevented the king's deer from getting onto the farm, but allowed an easy escape route.

The Dartmoor longhouse also came into being during this period. A longhouse was a rectangular, single-storey building constructed from granite, one room deep with a thatched roof. There were two entrances, located in the middle of each long side, and running between them was a central passage. One side of the passage was used by the humans and the other side was occupied by the animals. They both used the same doors.

The animal area was known as the shippon. This would have a stone drain running lengthways through the centre. The animals were tethered in a row with their heads facing the outside wall. They were tethered to wooden stakes which were fixed into granite slabs sunk into the ground. This design meant that the animals' backsides were neatly arranged over the central drain.

The living area had a central hearth for burning fires. There were no chimneys and the smoke would float up and drift through the thatched roof. If there were windows they were very small and possibly had shutters to keep out the draughts, so the interior would have been dark. The floors were packed-down earth, hard and cold, and the occupants would have slept around the fire to keep warm. Stores of corn were also probably kept in the living area as it was warm and dry, and the doors at either end of the cross-passage would create a breeze when open – which made it an ideal place for winnowing the corn (a method of separating the grain from the chaff, involving throwing the mixture into the air so the wind blows away the lighter chaff, while the heavier grains fall back down for recovery).

First modernisation began when sleeping platforms were built. A wooden frame was erected and planks were laid across, on which people would sleep. It was probably warmer up there but possibly rather smoky. Ladders were built to reach the platforms. Later, during the sixteenth and seventeenth centuries, further improvements were made with the construction of a stone chimney and a fireplace built beneath. Also around this time, the sleeping platform was extended to cover the whole room, thus creating a second storey; a staircase, rather than a ladder, was then added. Many farms built stone porches onto the entrance doors and some also added dairies.

Today you can see many longhouses on Dartmoor, three of which are only remains. If you wish to see ancient remains, the medieval village at Hound Tor is a wonderful example (*see* p.48).

There are 130 longhouses still in use today, either used as homes – modernised and equipped for today's lifestyle – or used as outbuildings. Most of the shippons have been converted into living quarters; however, there are a few that remain, one of which can be seen at Higher Uppacott, now owned by the Dartmoor National Park Authority. Here you can see the unaltered shippon and the original thatch, blackened by smoke.

THE LATE MIDDLE AGES

During the fourteenth century, it appears that many medieval settlements on the high moor were abandoned, probably due to a combination of the gradual change in climate (which affected crops and caused diseases in the cattle) and the Black Death. People moved to the warmer edges of the moor to settle and farm the lands there. During this time, sheep farming, wool, tin and rabbit warrening became the primary work of many people and played an important part in the prosperity of the many villages and settlements that were growing up around the edge of the moors.

These hamlets, villages and towns are there for you to see today, each unique, having developed in its own way around the moorland environment.

three

DARTMOOR INDUSTRY

GRANITE

The granite on Dartmoor has always been used by man. During the Bronze Age it was used to build shelters and beds, and also used for burials and sacred monuments. The moor was covered with granite boulders of all shapes and sizes and there was no need to quarry or cut it.

It wasn't until later that man developed a method to cut it and, as they did, more and more uses were found for it. Clapper bridges were built, boundary stones erected, crosses carved, houses built, walls put up, and troughs, apple crushers and cider presses cut out of it.

The first method of cutting granite was to make a groove along the rock with a metal tool and carve it deeper until the rock split. Later on, a number of holes were drilled in a row where the break was needed, one man holding a chisel and another hammering it in to the rock. Then they would drive in metal wedges until the rock split.

Towards the end of the nineteenth century, granite was used to lay roads. It was cut into small blocks, called setts, by men known as sett makers. Staple Tor was the source of the setts used in most of Plymouth's roads, whilst the cobblestones of Exeter came from Yeo and Chagford.

Because of its durability, granite became a popular building material not only on Dartmoor but throughout England. Foggintor Quarry near Princetown, and Haytor Quarry, became very busy supplying the granite for these buildings. The two quarries ended up being in competition over the years, but Haytor ended up being the main supplier to London because of its tramway connection to the canals.

STONE CROSSES

As you travel around Dartmoor you will spot many ancient stone crosses – in a churchyard, beside a track or on top of a tor – some obvious and some well hidden. They were carved from the granite and erected years ago for various reasons, either as village crosses or route markers, or perhaps as memorial stones.

I have included some of the crosses in this book, under the location where each is found, to aid those who wish to find them and to provide a brief background of the individual cross. They can be quite fascinating. There are several books written on stone crosses and a wonderful website giving more information if you would like to find out more. Please refer to the bibliography.

WATER

Over the centuries, the water on Dartmoor has provided its own inhabitants and the people from the surrounding lowlands with drinking water, a source of food, water for domestic use, a source of power and leisure activities such as swimming, fishing and canoeing. Its gurgling streams of clear water, rushing past moss-covered boulders and fern-lined banks, swirling around gnarled tree roots, also provide endless inspiration for photographers, artists, poets and daydreamers alike.

It was in the shallow, gravelly river-beds that tin was first discovered (*see* p.29) and water was essential to the industry. It was the tin miners who first diverted the water to make it suit their needs, by digging leats from a stream to where they needed it.

LEATS

You can still see leats on Dartmoor today, although there was once miles of them running across the area. In order to work they gently flowed downhill, but the downhill slope was very gradual so the water didn't move too fast. It was the engineering skills of the tin miners that led to this extensive use of leats.

Some leats took water to the surrounding cities and towns, some to industrial sites and some to dwellings which didn't have their own spring nearby. These leats were called pot water leats. Farm leats were built to supply farms with all their water needs, bringing water for the farmhouse and also for watering the animals, cleaning the parlour and for cooling purposes. A granite trough would be placed near the house and a constant flow of cold water running into the trough would keep the milk and cheese cool when placed in it.

Many of the leats are now dry but you can still see the course they took. There were some very long leats dug; the longest was the Plymouth Leat. The Plymouth Leat, also known as Drake's Leat, was built at the end of the sixteenth century to supply water to Plymouth (*see* p.86). This 18½-mile leat ran from the River Meavy to Plymouth and provided the inhabitants

'Irishmans Wall, Belstone.' (Mike Bartholomew)

'Leaning Wall at Foggintor Quarry.' (Miles Wolstenholme)

with water until the end of the 1700s, when the population grew and the Plymouth Docks, later known as Devonport, needed an extra supply. The Devonport Leat was constructed in the 1790s, which was even longer at 27 miles, to supply this other area of Plymouth. Its head (beginning) is just north of Wistman's Wood, and it now ends at Burrator Reservoir.

During the nineteenth century, Drake's Leat became insufficient as a water supply, especially as it clogged up and froze during the winter. In 1898, Burrator Reservoir was created to replace it. A dam was built and 117 acres of land were flooded. Later, in 1929, a further 150 acres were flooded, including some farms which are now at the bottom of the reservoir, their history lost. Other reservoirs were built on Dartmoor and now it supplies most of the surrounding area with water.

FARMING

Farming has taken place on Dartmoor since man first arrived, with reaves (*see* p.20) built during the Bronze Age to divide the land into fields for grazing and crops. As the climate changed, people moved off the high central moor to the lusher lowlands, and by the tenth century new fields and settlements were established on the edges of the moor with fields being narrow strips of land which were farmed collectively. Oats and barley, along with cattle and sheep, were the main crops during the Middle Ages.

By the middle of the thirteenth century, most of the central moorland was unenclosed grazing land, and a few farms, known as ancient tenements, were established – the tenants of which had full grazing rights over the forest. Between the forest and the enclosed lands lay the 'commons', which the farms in the parishes used for grazing.

Sheep were the most common domesticated animal in medieval times and wool was the most important industry in Devon. Dartmoor provided most of the sheep wool for the industry.

Today, the farming of sheep and cattle continues but the heavy rain, the low temperatures, harsh winds and poor soils mean that production per hectare is low.

PEAT

Dartmoor tenants and commoners had the right of 'turbary' – the right to take peat from the moor. At first, peat was used as fuel and the householders and farmers would dig it, stack it and dry it. When dry, it was burnt in their fireplaces, the slow burning and the wonderful smell making it perfect for keeping the home warm. Peat cutting was carried out during the summer months. Everybody would have their own area of land, known as a 'tie', to cut their peat from, and the farmer or householder would go back to his own tie every year. The turf was cut into slices known as turves, which were then stacked to dry out before they were burnt. Thatch roofs were built over the stacks to keep the rain off. Some of the peat was also taken by packhorse to the local town or village to sell.

During the nineteenth century, peat was used by the tinners to smelt ore in the blowing houses; the demand for it was so great that it soon became a small industry in itself. The tinners discovered that if it was converted to charcoal, it would give out even more heat, and there are a few humped mounds, or 'meilers', and granite kilns around Wild Tor which are a result of this process. Peat was transported mainly by packhorse to the mines.

At the same time, it was discovered that peat was a source of naphthalene and part of Princetown Prison, which at the time stood empty, was converted into a naphtha factory. In 1846, a tramway was built to bring the peat to Princetown and various methods were tried to extract the gas. They were all unsuccessful and the factory finally had to close.

Rattlebrook Head became an important peat works. In 1868 it was at its prime and a drying plant was set up. In 1878, a railway was built from Rattlebrook to the South West Railway at Bridestowe. The trucks were initially pulled by horses until, in 1930, a petrol-driven trolley was

'Bennetts Cross.' (Miles Wolstenholme)

'West Cleave, North Dartmoor.' (Miles Wolstenholme)

introduced. Peat extraction wasn't a success financially, so eventually the works closed down and the houses were destroyed by the army in 1961. Today you can follow the track of the railway and see the sleeper bridge where it crossed the Rattlebrook. You can also see the remains of the house known as Bleak House between Green Tor and Higher Dunnagoat. This was the manager's house, originally called Dunnagoat Cottage.

TIN MINING

When Dartmoor was being formed, vapours of certain minerals, including tin, flowed through the granite and became trapped in veins. The vapours cooled and condensed to form the tin and copper on Dartmoor. Over time, these veins were exposed, especially where streams and rivers ran over them, and the loose stones were washed down, accumulating on the outer edges of a bend in the stream.

TIN STREAMING

It is thought that tin was first discovered in streams during the twelfth century, and 'tin streaming' became the first method of tin extraction. The stones were dug out and placed to one side on the bank. The unwanted stones were put into a pile and usually formed a wall, behind which the precious tin ores were placed to prevent them rolling back into the stream. You can see the remains of this activity along many Dartmoor streams, where the heaps of rubble and waste have been overgrown with grass.

The large ore-bearing stones were then crushed into a powder, which was washed to remove the waste. Water from the streams was used to wash the waste away, and if the water wasn't running fast enough the miners would narrow the banks to speed up the flow. After years of this process, many rivers became silted up.

'Mine all Mine.' (Miles Wolstenholme)

OPEN-CAST MINING

Later on, the miners would look for the lode – the vein of ore – and dig it out directly. This was known as 'open-cast mining'. The stones were still crushed and washed and, if there wasn't a stream in the immediate area for the washing process, the miners would build a leat from the nearest stream to bring the water to where it was needed. Tin miners became expert leat builders and were consulted by Sir Francis Drake prior to the construction of the Plymouth Leat (*see* p.86).

TIN SMELTING

The next stage in the process was smelting. Once the tin (known as black tin) had been extracted, it was smelted to form white tin. The first method used to smelt tin was to dig a hole in the ground and light a fire in it. The tin was put in the fire. When the fire went out, the pure white tin was picked from the ashes. The process was later improved by building cones, which served as a furnace. The fire was lit at the bottom of the narrow end with a space below it. The tin was once again put in the fire and would drop into the bottom of the cone.

BLOWING HOUSES

In the fourteenth century, blowing houses were invented – the next progression in tin smelting. They were small huts with thatched roofs, usually located beside a stream, and were supplied with water by a leat which ran from upstream and would power a waterwheel on the side of the hut. The water then ran back into the stream below. The waterwheel powered a pair of huge bellows which would keep the furnace alight.

Inside the blowing house was a granite furnace with granite rafters laid over a granite basin. The fire was built on top of the rafters, the charcoal and black tin being placed in layers. When this was lit and burning hot enough (with the help of the bellows), the smelted tin would drop through the rafters into the basin below. It was then ladled out into granite moulds which held between 200 and 300lbs of tin. These tin ingots were then taken to the nearest stannary town for weighing and checking.

SHAFT MINING

It wasn't until the eighteenth century that deep mining was used on Dartmoor, and the early mines were shallow because there was such a risk of flooding on the moors. Shafts were dug down to the lode and a kibble (an iron bucket) was lowered down using a wrench. The bucket was filled with the mined stones and wound back up.

Drainage adits (horizontal tunnels used to drain the water away) were one method used to deal with flooding, and this was soon replaced by pumping out the water. Waterwheels and then steam engines were used to operate the pumps. There are no waterwheels remaining on high Dartmoor but evidence of their use can be seen in the wheelpits that are found at various sites.

Initially the crushing process involved a mechanised stamp, powered by a waterwheel, but a more sophisticated method was developed to wash the waste away. A circular pool was dug and water was run into it, where a device called a buddle would separate the waste out. Tin mining continued at certain sites until well into the twentieth century.

CLAY

China clay, also known as kaolin, is a component of granite which was formed when Dartmoor first came into being (*see* p.11). The working of china clay developed in the eighteenth century, when William Cookworthy discovered a method of using kaolin to make hard porcelain, similar to that produced in China. The clay was extracted by removing the layer of peat from it and then mixing it with water. The water would turn milky and run along into settling pits – the heavier, unwanted sand being left behind. The clay in the water would settle whilst in the pits and then the water was carefully drained off, leaving the clay behind. This was dug out and dried. Today the principle is the same but the process has been modernised.

Over the years, there have been various small pits for working china clay on the moor, but the major developments are now concentrated in the south-west. Lee Moor is still in operation today. China clay is the most important modern geological product from around Dartmoor. Only a small amount of clay is used for ceramics today, with around 75 per cent used for various other purposes, such as for fertilisers, paint, medicines and plastics, and whitener and coating in the manufacture of paper.

four

DARTMOOR WILDLIFE HABITATS

Dartmoor supports various wildlife habitats with some interesting and sometimes rare species of plant and animal life. This unusual mix gives Dartmoor its beauty and uniqueness. Here are some of the species found in each habitat, and the page number on which you can find more information:

BLANKET BOG

The two highest areas on Dartmoor are covered with peat blanket bog, which is nutrient-poor and wet. Plants found growing here include: deer grass, hare's tail cottongrass, cross leaved heath (*see* p.116), round leaved sundew (*see* p.125), bog asphodel (*see* p.136) and bog mosses.

The only animals that live here are the dunlin (*see* p.116) and the golden plover (*see* p.116).

UPLAND HEATH

Surrounding the blanket bogs, this is a mixture of heath and grasses. The main plant found here is ling, but there is also bell heather (*see* p.101), bilberry (*see* p.58), western gorse (*see* p.83) and, in the wetter areas, cross leaved heath (*see* p.116) and purple moor grass (*see* p.141).

Animals living here include meadow pipits (*see* p.65), stonechats (*see* p.72), skylarks (*see* p.150), adders (*see* p.150), lizards (*see* p.132), the emperor moth caterpillar, red grouse (*see* p.57) and ring ouzel (*see* p.104).

GRASS MOOR

This grassy moorland is formed of bent and fescues which create a short, stubby mat which becomes dotted with tormentil (*see* p.85), bedstraw (*see* p.48) and milkwort flowers (*see* p.150). Grass and bracken (*see* p.56) grow on the drier slopes.

The main animals living here are the cattle, sheep and ponies out to graze; the wild animals include voles, wheatears (*see* p.96), whinchats, the small heath butterfly and the brown and pearl-bordered fritillary butterfly (in some bracken areas).

TORS AND ROCKY OUTCROPS

A Dartmoor tor typically supports up to sixty different lichens, some of which are more commonly found in the Arctic. Birds that nest up here include ravens (*see* p.67), ring ouzels (*see* p.104), peregrine falcons (*see* p.129) and wheatears (*see* p.96).

'Redwater Brook.' (Miles Wolstenholme)

VALLEY MIRE

This is the wet marshy area found around some rivers. Plants growing here are cotton grass, cross leaved heath (*see* p.116), bogbean (*see* p.118), pale butterwort, sedges and bog mosses.

The animal species here are the dragonfly, snipe (*see* p.135) and curlew.

UPLAND OAK WOODLANDS

These ancient woodlands are found on steep river valleys or in areas covered with boulders. They are predominantly oak, but also found here are birch, hazel (*see* p.76), holly (*see* p.130), rowan (*see* p.145) and abundant ferns, mosses and lichens growing on the boulders and the branches.

Animals found here include the insect-eating pied flycatcher (*see* p.129), wood warbler (*see* p.139) and redstart (*see* p.110), along with woodmice (*see* p.95), dormice, grey squirrels (*see* p.154), badgers (*see* p.131), wood ants (*see* p.140) and the blue ground beetle.

PLANTATION WOODLANDS

Not much grows here other than the planted species, which include exotic conifers, Sitka spruce or Norway spruce.

The animals living here – the crossbill and the nightjar – are not common to the moors but are specific to this habitat.

ENCLOSED FARMLAND

The enclosed farmland on the edges of the granite mass provides another variety of habitat. The areas of Rhos pasture support the devil's-bit scabious, the heath spotted orchid (*see* p.70) and the ivy-leaved bell flower.

The animal life found here includes the marsh fritillary butterfly, the narrow-bordered bee hawk-moth, snipe, (*see* p.135) reed bunting (*see* p.104), foxes and roe deer (*see* p.142).

In the hay meadows grow oxeye daisy (*see* p.116), red clover, yellow rattle, knap weed and the rare butterfly orchids.

HEDGEBANKS AND STONEWALLS

The stone walls and hedgebanks on the outskirts of Dartmoor are very old, and growing here you will find hawthorn (*see* p.147), blackthorn (*see* p.129), hazel (*see* p.76), oak (*see* p.86), ash, red campion (*see* p.52), greater stitchwort (*see* p.45), navelwort and ferns. Living in this habitat are the song thrush, yellowhammer (*see* p.79) and whitethroats (*see* p.75), and buzzards (*see* p.118) nest in the trees.

Although farmland cannot truly be called wild habitat, it is still one of the most important habitats in Britain for wildlife – especially if hedges and trees grow around the fields. Fields, hedges and the heathlands of Dartmoor and the UK exist because they have been created and managed by people. If left alone, these areas would turn back to woodland. If a garden was left untended it would soon be taken over by small shrubs like bramble, which in turn would be replaced by fast-growing trees such as ash and sycamore. Finally, beech and oak trees would dominate. These changes in plant life within a habitat are called 'succession' and, if left alone by humans, continue until a climax is reached. Oak woodland is the commonest climax vegetation in Britain.

How to Work Out the Age of a Hedge

Hedges were first planted by the Anglo-Saxons and some are hundreds of years old. The most common hedgerow plant was the hawthorn, but hedges now contain many species of shrub, some planted on purpose and others seeding over time. You are likely to spot the following in a Dartmoor hedge: hawthorn, blackthorn, hazel, ash, beech, holly, oak, sycamore, rowan and elder.

Many hedges have a bank or strip of grassland underneath them where many varieties of flower and grass grow, including ferns, primroses, foxgloves, red campion, stitchwort and cow parsley.

You can work out the approximate age of a hedge relatively easily. In an old hedgerow, one new species of shrub establishes itself roughly every 100 years. So, if you take a 30m stretch of a hedgerow and list the number of different species you find within it, and multiply by 100 years, you will have an idea of how old it is. To get an accurate result, a thorough search for the various species is necessary, and this method doesn't work for newer hedges.

TORRENT RIVERS AND STREAM

Not much lives in the fast flowing, rapidly rising and falling torrent rivers of Dartmoor but, where the water stops in a side channel, mosses, liverworts, algae and floating weeds live. Along the riverbanks grow the royal fern and the lemon-scented fern. In the waters are fish such as trout and salmon, which live off the insect larvae; other animals living here are the dipper, the heron, goosander, grey wagtail and otters.

RESERVOIRS

A man-made phenomenon, the reservoirs only support plants that can manage when the water is high or low. These plants include rushes, reeds and various waterplants. Fish have been introduced to the reservoirs and frogs, toads, newts and leeches breed here. Birds found here include cormorants and wintering wild ducks.

five

DARTMOOR PONIES

On Dartmoor you will see ponies everywhere – grazing on the commons, drinking from the streams, galloping in herds across the open moor, on postcards, in books and on the shelves of every souvenir shop on the moor. They have become symbolic of Dartmoor and visitors travel here specifically to see the ponies running wild and free. Even the Dartmoor National Park Authority uses a pony for their logo. However, the ponies of Dartmoor aren't actually wild. They are all owned by somebody on the moors and you can usually see their owner's mark on their coats.

Ponies were brought to the West Country by Phoenician traders 2,000 years ago and they evolved into two breeds: Exmoor and Dartmoor. The first written record of the horse on Dartmoor was in AD 1012, when the rounding up of the 'wild horses' of Ashburton was recorded in manorial records, indicating that many ponies remained unbroken but were branded as belonging to somebody.

Initially, ponies were used on the farms and to transport families to and from church and the market, then they were used more and more in the local industries. The peat cutters would use ponies as packhorses to transport peat over the moors and, as tin mining grew, even more ponies were used. They were loaded with bags of tin ingots on either side and would travel in groups across the moors to the stannary towns. The granite quarry also used ponies, to pull the trucks up and down the granite railway from Haytor Quarries to the quayside at Teigngrace, where the granite was loaded onto the barges to be taken to London. When the mines were closed some of the ponies were kept for farming, but most of them were left to roam free.

During the 1900s, man started to influence the breeding of the pony and certain breeds of horse were mated with the Dartmoor, producing various qualities. Arabs and Fell ponies were introduced to produce the characteristics required for a good Polo pony, and the Prince of Wales founded the Duchy Stud near Princetown to breed suitable ponies. Shetland ponies were also introduced to produce sturdy, tough animals for the coal mining pits of the north, some of which never saw the light of day once they started their work.

In 1925, the Dartmoor Pony Society was formed in order to register the ponies of Dartmoor and preserve the indigenous quality of the pure Dartmoor pony. No longer was the pony native and running free; it was a recognised breed with qualities governed by man. Consequently, today you can see several breeds of pony on Dartmoor:

- The 'native' pony – the most common breed – which is a mix of all the ponies on the moor; their parentage is unknown. This type of pony is now recognised as a rare breed by the Rare Breeds Survival Trust.

'Ponies in
Bracken.' (Miles
Wolstenholme)

'Ponies Nose
to Nose.' (Miles
Wolstenholme)

'Pony and
Foal.' (Miles
Wolstenholme)

- The 'pure bred', or registered Dartmoor pony, has a recorded pedigree. Its parents are chosen and breeding is controlled. The pure breed is more refined and not usually seen out on the moors – partly because it is too valuable and partly to prevent uncontrolled breeding with unregistered ponies. This is the Dartmoor pony that is found at pony breed shows.
- The Shetland pony can also be found on Dartmoor. It was introduced in the early twentieth century to produce the small, hardy cross-breeds for the mines. They are well suited to the tough Dartmoor environment.

RUNNING FREE

Although they aren't really wild, the ponies of Dartmoor live out on the moors all year round, roaming the moors in herds, grazing on the stubby moorland grass. You will see the herds sticking together, a group of mares with one adult stallion and young ponies and foals. The foals are born between May and August and are often the cause of traffic hold-ups as excited tourists stop to take photographs. Ponies frequently wander onto the road, as do the sheep and cattle, and motorists have to stop suddenly to avoid hitting them. Unfortunately, some don't stop and there are numerous pony deaths every year.

Do not feed the ponies on Dartmoor, even if they seem to want food; it encourages them to wander onto the road and is the cause of so many deaths.

THE PONY DRIFT

Every year in September the annual pony drift takes place. All of the ponies on the moors are rounded up by people on horseback, quads and on foot, and herded into a field or farmyard. Here they are sorted into groups according to owners. Ownership is easy to ascertain as they are branded on their coats. Any sick ponies are treated, and those that are too ill or too old to go back out on the moors for another year are separated out. The owners may also decide to sell some of their ponies, and these are kept back whilst the remaining healthy and strong ponies are returned to roam wild for another year.

The pony drift has taken place every year for centuries and was originally a way to sort out ponies which were set out to graze illegally. The first written record of a pony drift was in AD 1012, and in 1608 it was agreed at a Court of Survey held at Lydford that there should be three summer drifts and one winter drift.

The Forest of Dartmoor was divided into quarters in those days and each quarter was managed by a 'moorman' who paid rent to the Duchy of Cornwall for the land. Each quarter was further divided up and sublet to other moormen, who would pay rent to the main moorman. These moormen would charge the local farmers and animal keepers to look after the animals, which were brought up to graze during the summer. The moormen organised the drifts every year; they took place on different days in each quarter and there would deliberately be no advance notice, so that those illegally grazing animals didn't have the chance to remove them.

The ponies were rounded up and herded from the forest into pounds, an area enclosed by a stone wall; each quarter had its own pound. Creber Pound was for the north quarter, Dunnabridge Pound for the east, Laugh Tor Pound was used in conjunction with Dunnabridge Pound, and Erne Pound was for the south quarter. The ponies were then picked up by their owners, and the owners of any ponies which weren't supposed to be in the forest were fined. If after three days the ponies weren't claimed, they were taken to Lydford Pound and, if they still weren't claimed after three weeks, then they were considered to be the property of the Duchy and were sold.

Dunnabridge Pound was originally a Bronze Age enclosure and was later used for the pony drifts. Inside the wall, next to the gate, a stone-built chair called Dinah's Chair can be seen. Dinah and Sam Tuckett ran the pound and were known for their refusal to bend the rules – especially Dinah, who reputedly sent many a farmer packing if he didn't have the fine to pay for the release of his ponies.

AFTER THE DRIFT TODAY

Before modern machinery and transport it was easy to sell ponies, as they were needed for transport, to pull carts and ploughs, and for packhorses. However, as everything became mechanised, the demand for ponies dropped and they were exported to Europe for consumption by humans.

Later, the ban on exporting live animals put an end to this market, so now other markets are being explored and the ponies are sold for riding ponies and for conservation grazers. Dartmoor ponies have very gentle natures and make wonderful riding ponies for children. They are also used in show jumping, as working ponies and to drive carriages.

PRESERVATION OF THE PONIES

Today there are fewer than 1,500 ponies on Dartmoor, compared to 30,000 in 1950, and several groups have been established to protect the future of the Dartmoor pony and promote the pony to markets further afield:

THE DARTMOOR PONY HERITAGE TRUST

A registered charity dedicated to the preservation of the native Dartmoor pony breed. The unregistered Dartmoor pony numbers have dropped to a critical level, and if they are lost from Dartmoor then the breed will be considered extinct. A new pony centre has been opened at Parke, the head office of the Dartmoor National Park Authority.

THE DARTMOOR PONY TRAINING CENTRE

Originally called the Dartmoor Pony Rescue Centre, this group was established in 2005 to take on ponies which weren't sold at the markets, or ponies going to dealers for low prices. It is a non-profit voluntary organisation, training and rehoming these ponies, preferably to do high-profile jobs such as working with people with special needs.

THE FRIENDS OF THE DARTMOOR HILL PONY ASSOCIATION

This group provides information on all the ponies and promotes the Dartmoor pony with the aim of increasing its value and expanding the market. The organisation also provides up-to-date information about the drift sales and will help people to buy and transport their pony home.

THE DARTMOOR PONY SOCIETY

The main role of this society is to maintain the Stud Book, which holds records of all the pure bred Dartmoor ponies. Originally these records were held in the Polo Pony Stud Book, then in the books of the National Pony Society and, thirty years ago, the Dartmoor Pony Society took over. Now they issue all the foal registrations, transfers and re-entries into the Stallion and Geldings section each year.

SIX

DARTMOOR: A NATIONAL PARK

National Parks were born in America when an immigrant Scotsman named John Muir peti-tioned the United States Congress for the National Parks Bill, which led to the world's first National Park being established at Yellowstone on 1 March 1872. John Muir is today thought of as the 'Father of National Parks'.

The first National Parks to be designated in Europe were in Sweden on 24 May 1909. The development of National Parks in the UK can be traced over a period of 150 years. Early interest was expressed by romantic poets, such as William Wordsworth, who famously claimed that the Lake District was 'a sort of national property, in which every man has a right and an interest who has an eye to perceive and a heart to enjoy'. Until then, remote and relatively wild areas had been seen as somewhat uncivilised and dangerous.

The popularity of access to the countryside increased during the Industrial Revolution, as individuals sought out a breathing space, free from the noise and clamour of heavy industry. The years between the First and Second World Wars saw the pressure for access to England's 'green and pleasant land' increase, culminating in the 1932 Kinder mass-trespass by a splinter group of ramblers in what is now the Peak District National Park. A number of the group were imprisoned.

At the end of the Second World War, as part of the post-war reconstruction effort, the govern-ment set up committees to examine long-term land use, the availability of land for recreational use, and nature conservation.

John Dower, an architect and rambler, was asked to report on how the National Park ideal could work for England and Wales. His report, and the subsequent Hobhouse report of 1947, paved the way for National Parks in the UK.

In 1949, the National Parks and Access to the Countryside Act was passed, and the first National Parks were designated in 1951. Dartmoor was designated that year – the fourth area of land in the UK to receive National Park status.

The UK's National Parks are part of a global family of over 113,000 protected areas, covering 149 million square km, or 6 per cent of the Earth's surface. National Parks cover 10 per cent of the UK's rural areas, with a combined resident population in excess of 270,000, and play a vital role in safeguarding nature, wildlife and landscapes.

Although 'national' in the sense that it is of special value because of its natural beauty, cultural heritage and the recreational opportunities it offers to all, Dartmoor is not nationally owned. The landscape of the National Park has been created by farmers and landowners over thousands of years and today most of the land remains in their hands. Dartmoor National Park Authority exists to secure for the public good the conservation, enhancement, enjoyment and understanding of the special qualities of Dartmoor, its landscape, wildlife and cultural heritage. Its role is clearly defined by Parliament in the two statutory purposes of National Parks:

- to conserve and enhance the natural beauty, wildlife and cultural heritage of the area
- to promote opportunities for the understanding and enjoyment of the area's special qualities by the public

In pursuing these purposes, the National Park Authority also has a duty to try to foster the economic and social well-being of the communities within the National Park. Conserving and enhancing Dartmoor's environment provides a huge range of benefits that are beyond monetary value. These benefits include:

- A landscape of international importance
- A wildlife, geological and cultural heritage, also of international importance, and, in the case of geological and archaeological resources and the historic-built environment, finite rural traditions and ways of life
- Helping meet the water needs of the region
- Storage of huge quantities of CO_2 in the peats and organic soils of Dartmoor
- Capturing of CO_2 from the atmosphere (carbon sequestration) through the blanket bogs of Dartmoor in particular, but also through its woods and vegetation cover more generally
- An unrivalled recreation resource for relaxation and escape in natural surroundings
- Contributing to the region's health and well-being
- Providing an outdoor classroom

In order to deliver these benefits, Dartmoor National Park Authority works in partnership with everyone who has an interest in Dartmoor, from national agencies and local authorities to local communities, the voluntary sector and visitors.

The Dartmoor National Park Authority employs specialist officers, including archaeologists, ecologists, arboriculturalists, planning officers and historic-building specialists to help care for Dartmoor's biodiversity, landscapes, special habitats and cultural heritage. The Authority also employs tourism, information, education and communications specialists, who work to promote understanding and enjoyment of the National Park. A team of rangers provide practical support and carry out vital liaison work with local communities, and a specialist works team undertakes practical conservation projects.

Funding for the work carried out by the National Park Authority comes from central government, and from fees and charges. The role of Dartmoor National Park Authority and its partners will become of ever greater importance as the regional and urban population grows, rates of change in the wider world accelerate, and the need for breathing spaces such as Dartmoor National Park increases.

seven

DARTMOOR SETTLEMENTS AND THEIR SURROUNDING AREAS

EAST DARTMOOR

MORETONHAMPSTEAD

Moretonhampstead originated as a small Saxon settlement around AD 700. The name comes from 'Mortun', a Saxon word meaning 'enclosed piece of land near the moor'. 'Hampstead' comes from one of the many Lords of the Manor.

The present parish spreads over 6,000 acres. The manor of Moreton, along with some neighbouring manors, used to support over 5,000 sheep, and for 700 years the main industry of the town was wool and the manufacture of woollen cloth. A water-powered fulling mill was built in the thirteenth century, indicating that the wool industry must have been well established by that time.

In 1207, King John granted the town a weekly market and an annual five-day fair, and the local economy boomed until the end of the seventeenth century when the wool industry declined. The town then became a local trading centre and watering hole for Dartmoor travellers.

Today, Moretonhampstead is a thriving town with a selection of shops, pubs, accommodation, a hospital, library, swimming pool and many small businesses. It is home to many potters and artists and there are many sculptures of local wildlife to be found. There are several interesting historical sites.

The Cross Tree

One site with an interesting story behind it is what is known as the Cross Tree, which can be found on the way to the Church of St Andrews. The Cross Tree was originally the site of a market cross standing on church land. After the Reformation, the cross fell into disuse. Some time later, by chance, an elm seed germinated in the bowl that held the cross. Because nobody took care of the cross, the elm began to grow until eventually its roots grew so big that they caused the cross to fall and break. The base was probably taken and used as a gatepost, or put to some other use, but the cross still remains today. The tree grew without interference until 1799, when the London Inn and Tavern was opened and the owner decided to pollard the tree, giving it the appearance of a punch bowl. The tree was then given its other name, the Punchbowl Tree. It became a centre for town celebrations and, on special occasions such as May Day, much of the merry-making took place around the tree. It then gained another name, the Dancing Tree.

By 1862, the tree was a bit of a tourist attraction and a well-known symbol of Moretonhampstead. But tragically, on 13 October 1891, a violent storm hit the town and most of the tree was toppled. An attempt was made to save the tree and it survived a further twelve years until another storm completely destroyed it. Eventually, a copper beech was planted in the same place and this is what you will see today.

The Sparrowhawk at Moretonhampstead. (Author's collection)

The Church of St Andrew

Situated on high ground adjoining the Sentry, the parish church, dedicated to St Andrew, dates from around 1450. It is a very impressive church with a massive church tower and stair turret. When the church was first restored, it appears that many things were removed and a fine oak screen was thrown out – luckily recovered by the Earl of Devon, who gave it to Whitchurch near Tavistock. In 1901, the church was enlarged and improved by Viscount Hambledon, who had an organ chamber built along with a vestry and a new screen. He also built a Rectory next to the Sentry, although it is no longer used as such.

The Almshouses

Now owned by the National Trust, this two-storey granite building was constructed in 1451 as a hospital. It is the most notable building in Moretonhampstead, with its attractive series of columns spanning the front. In 1637 it was refurbished into eight single-room dwellings, separated by oak plank and muntin screens. Screens of this type were common internal features of late medieval buildings, but they became rarer as architecture progressed and living space was sectioned into ever smaller and more discreet rooms.

During the eighteenth century the building was used as a workhouse, and then in the nineteenth century it was converted into four one-up one-down dwellings. In 1938, the whole building was purchased by a Mr Davie of Hayne, who presented it to the town along with a trust he had created for them. In 1952, the building was purchased by the National Trust.

The Sparrowhawk

Swooping down from a wall in the town square you will see the sparrowhawk. This was created by artist Roger Dean. Its story originates from when King John granted the town its charter in the thirteenth century and set the rent as one sparrowhawk per year.

The Sentry

Next to the churchyard lies a park-like enclosure which is used by the town as a recreation field. It was originally owned by the church and was known as the Sanctuary Field; such fields were originally there for rectors to earn a profit from. This one, however, was used for years as a recreation field by the local community and especially the children.

That was until 1837, when the rector at the time, William Courtenay Clack, pointed out to the villagers that the field was in fact owned by the Church. He announced that he wanted to make a profit from it and would be taking a crop of hay that year – therefore the children were no longer welcome. You can imagine the uproar. An action group was established and fought legally for their rights to use the field, but this made Clack block the paths to the field and caused more disruption. In the end, the church bell ringers didn't turn up to ring, the choir didn't turn up to sing and even the church pews were empty. Finally, the Earl of Devon stepped in and the villagers' rights were restored.

However, in 1907 the newest rector, Stanley Dawes Dewey, decided he didn't like paying for the upkeep of a recreational field for his parishioners. So, he erected a barbed wire fence around the field. The matter was eventually resolved when the Newton Abbot Rural District Council took action under the Barbed Wire Act of 1893, which made it illegal to obstruct a right of way with barbed wire.

NORTH BOVEY

A picturesque village about 1½ miles from Moretonhampstead, North Bovey consists of a village green, a pub, a cluster of thatched cottages and some modern rows of slated-roof terraces.

During the fourteenth and fifteenth centuries, North Bovey was a prosperous tin mining village with both open-cast and shaft workings. The tithes from the mining were used to build the church.

Towards the end of the nineteenth century, the decline of tin mining left the village with a dwindling prosperity. However, its fortunes changed when W.H. Smith bought the land from the former Earl of Devon. In 1891, his son Frederick inherited the estate and built himself a modest family home just outside of the village – now the Bovey Castle Hotel. Frederick invested in the village, renovating farms and houses, and even built the rows of terraced homes for his estate workers. The population then was around 600.

Now the population is around 250. There is no longer a post office, no longer a school and no children playing on the village green. Most of the properties are second homes and are mainly empty, but it is a wonderful base for a Dartmoor walking holiday. The Ring O' Bells pub is a very popular place to eat, and its cosy olde worlde atmosphere makes it well worth a visit.

Bovey Castle

Bovey Castle was originally built by Frederick Smith (son of W.H. Smith). The building was finished in 1907 and became known as the Manor House. Since then, the house has been used as a convalescent home during the First World War and then as a military hospital in 1939 when war broke out again. From 1946–83, it was returned to the Great Western Railway and reopened as a hotel. In 1991, its new owners expanded it considerably and the golf course became the top priority. In 2003 the building was named Bovey Castle.

MANATON

The parish of Manaton includes much open moorland, as well as the village itself, and contains a cross section of all the geographical features for which Dartmoor is famous, from high moorland, through rocky tors, cultivated uplands, broadleaf woodland to steep river valleys. The lowest elevation of the parish is on the River Bovey at 75m, and the highest on Hameldown at 530m. The village of Manaton is renowned as a starting point for some of the best walks on Dartmoor.

The first settlement in the area was at Grimspound, which is a Bronze Age enclosed hut group with twenty-four huts and some livestock pens. It is one of the most outstanding Bronze Age sites in Britain today.

By the time of the Domesday Book, 1086, there appear to have been several flourishing settlements in the Manaton parish, the best known being the medieval village at Hound Tor, just

North Bovey. (Author's collection)

below Greater Rocks. The village was abandoned sometime in the fourteenth century, probably due to the Black Death (1349), or perhaps as a result of climate change making it harder to grow crops on the moor. The populations then gathered in Manaton, Freelands and Water, forming what is today's village of Manaton.

Manaton Show and Fair

Every August on a Saturday, Manaton hosts its popular village show with all the usual country village activities and more. Arts and crafts, home produce, a tug-of-war competition, ferret racing, dog shows, children's entertainment, welly throwing and much more takes place, and the village comes alive with merry-making.

St Winifred's Church

The church at Manaton dates back to the fifteenth century. It is situated next to the village green and there are two fascinating stories attached to it:

The Manaton Storm

Back in 1779, the people of Manaton were becoming increasingly unhappy with their clergyman. He was disliked by most people and was only supposed to be there on a temporary basis. His idea of temporary was far longer than most other people's, though, and there was unrest amongst the parishioners.

However, fate took a hand in matters when, on 13 December, a violent storm swept across the moor and a huge bolt of lightning struck the church tower, splitting it off from its base. Fortunately it was a Monday, and there was nobody inside when the huge pinnacle came crashing through the roof of the nave, damaging the belfry, the bell wheels and even the altar.

The villagers thought this must be a sign from God, telling them he wasn't happy with the way they had been conducting their lives. Feeling reprimanded, they changed their ways for a little while and stopped frequenting the pub. However, it wasn't long before the clergyman was blamed, and the villagers became convinced it was God telling him to move on.

It appears that this greatly affected the clergyman too; he became ill and took to his bed. During his time off, he made up his mind to resign from his post; however, God had other plans for him and he died before he was able to resign.

The Heathen Cross of Manaton

Another strange story of Manaton church dates back to the years when a coffin coming into the churchyard was traditionally carried three times around the church cross in a sunwise (clockwise) direction. The ritual supposedly originated from the days of the 'old Gods' and every villager burying a relative would make sure they observed the tradition, believing it would bring unrest to the soul if they didn't.

Tradition was peacefully adhered to until 1841, when Revd Charles Carwithin, the new vicar in the village, decided it was actually a pagan ritual and gently tried to persuade his parishioners of the error of their ways. They didn't listen, as the fear of not doing it was stronger than fear of the wrath of God, so the vicar started preaching about the sins of the heathen and of pagan practices being carried out in the sanctity of his graveyard.

Much to the relief of the villagers, the vicar eventually went quiet on the matter. Then, one day it was discovered that the church cross had gone. Immediately the search began for the cross, but it had completely disappeared. It was rumoured that the vicar had smashed it to pieces one night, but there was no proof. Seven years later the vicar left the parish, and still no light was shed on the subject.

Sixty years later, in 1908, a workman who was carrying out repairs to the church tower was strolling past the nearby stream when he noticed a huge slab of granite holding up a wall which crossed over the stream. Looking closer, he realised that the slab was actually a church cross! A work party removed it from the stream and carried it to the churchyard with the intention of reuniting it with its base. Much to their astonishment, it didn't fit – it wasn't their church cross at all. However, the vicar decided that any church cross was better than no church cross and so it still stands there today, looking too big for its base.

Greater Stitchwort (*Stellaria holostea*)

This delicate white flower is profuse in Dartmoor hedgerows and grows alongside the red campion.

Jay's Grave

One of the most well-known stories on Dartmoor, and one of the most visited sites, is that of Jay's Grave. The story starts in 1790, when an orphaned baby girl was taken to the poor house in Newton Abbot where she was named Mary Jay. She grew up in the poor house until she was in her teens, then was sent to work on Canna Farm near Manaton. Here she had an even harder life, working in the house and in the fields with long days and few decent meals or warm clothes. Here they called her Kitty Jay.

When the farmer's son started paying her attention she was flattered, as it was the only bit of affection she had ever had. Unfortunately she became pregnant. The farmer and his wife couldn't face the truth and told everybody that she had thrown herself at their son. She was thrown off the farm and left with a ruined reputation. With no hope of finding other employment, and only the prospect of returning to the poor house, Kitty Jay could see no future ahead of her and hung herself in Canna Barn.

In those days, nobody who took their own life could be buried in sacred ground; they were usually buried at a crossroads, preferably on the parish boundary. In that way, their soul had less chance of returning to its home ground to haunt anybody. Kitty Jay was buried at the intersection of a road and an old moorland miners' track. The grave became known as Jay's Grave.

It wasn't long before strange things started happening at the grave. On certain moonlit nights, a dark figure would appear and kneel beside the grave with its head in its hands – and it still does to this day. Some say it is the soul of the farmer's son, begging for forgiveness.

The other rather strange occurrence is that every day there are fresh flowers on the grave. Nobody knows who places them there and nobody has seen anybody doing it. Some believe it is the Dartmoor piskies, who will tend the grave until eternity.

The grave was later dug up by Mr James Bryant and it was confirmed that the bones within were female. He buried them once again in the same spot and erected a headstone. Now the grave is adorned with flowers and gifts from well-wishers and has become a place of pilgrimage, with songs and poems written about the tragedy of poor Kitty Jay.

Bowerman's Nose

Bowerman's Nose is an odd-looking column of rocks standing on the moor close to Manaton. It resembles a man and, if you believe what the legends say, then it seems that it once *was* a man – Bowerman the Hunter.

Many years ago, Bowerman, a tall and powerful man whose main passion in life was hunting, lived on the moors. He would ride across the moors with the fiercest pack of hounds ever seen on Dartmoor and most people were in awe of him. In fact, he was a very popular man known for his generosity and kindness; everybody liked him. Everybody, that is, except for the witches. The witches despised him.

Witches were allegedly a common problem on Dartmoor at that time, gathering together to brew spells and summon up mists – generally terrifying the local inhabitants. Their cackling laughter would send a chill down your spine, as you knew some poor soul had been lured to his death in the bogs. Well, Bowerman wasn't scared of witches and he encouraged others not be afraid of them. As you can imagine, the witches didn't like this at all.

One day, a group of witches were huddled around a fire, brewing up wicked spells and chanting incantations, when Bowerman passed close by with his pack of hounds. The hounds picked up the scent of a hare and instantly set off after it and, unluckily for the witches, the hare rushed down the pass where they were clustered. It dashed through their huddle at full speed, followed by the crazed pack of hounds, and finally by Bowerman himself, who shouted with hilarity as the witches were thrown into chaos with the cauldron and wands flying in all directions.

Furious, the witches gathered together and decided that Bowerman was definitely going to pay for his conduct. They knew he would have to return past them as the track led to a dead end, so they plotted that Levera, a witch who could turn herself into any animal, would change into a hare and lead Bowerman into an ambush. Bowerman and his pack soon returned, and the hounds picked up the scent of Levera and started a new chase. This chase turned out to be the longest they had ever given. Through woods, across streams, around tors, through marshes and mires and over rocky outcrops until, exhausted, Bowerman and his pack rounded a tor and came across the evil witches. Within a flash he was surrounded, and together the witches summoned all their power and cast a mighty spell, turning Bowerman and his pack to stone.

To this day they stand there, Bowerman towering above his pack of hounds, the cluster of scattered boulders around him.

'Jay's Grave.'
(Miles Wolstenholme)

'Bowerman's Nose.'
(Mike Bartholomew)

'Hound Tor.'
(Mike Bartholomew)

Heath Bedstraw (*Galium saxatile*)

This perennial matt-forming herb is found on grassland and moors. It is low growing and can reach a height of 20cm. You can see its white flowers from May to August.

Hound Tor

Hound Tor is one of the most well-known tors on Dartmoor. Supposedly the inspiration behind Conan Doyle's *The Hound of the Baskervilles*, the Domesday Book records the name of the tor as 'Hundatora', taking its name from the word 'hound'.

Stunning in appearance, consisting of two huge separate rock masses, it is an example of a Dartmoor 'avenue tor', with the highest point being 414m. In October 1995, one of the towering stacks of rock crashed over. Nobody knows why. It was estimated that 500 tons of granite crashed from the tor.

The tor is a popular place to visit and is a fashionable climbing and bouldering destination. Bouldering is a form of rock climbing without ropes, which is usually limited to short climbs over a crash pad (bouldering mattress). The other popular attraction at Hound Tor is the van 'The Hound of the Basket Meals', well-known for its food and drink.

Hound Tor is also famed for its ghosts, and there have been many sightings. Years ago, a school master suddenly had a heart seizure whilst walking amongst the rocks. During his fit, he started to speak in Hebrew – which he had never before spoken. He died three days later. It is said that he saw the ghost of one of the Jewish men who used to work in the mines there. There have also been many reported sightings of a black dog that appears and vanishes at will.

There is plenty of archaeological evidence around Hound Tor to indicate that the area was lived in from the late Neolithic to Early Bronze Age periods. On the east side of the tor is a low stony bank running between the two outcrops – the remains of a Neolithic tor enclosure. On the north side are the remains of an enclosure containing a hut circle, and on the west is a cairn containing a kist and a retaining kerb circle. On the open moorland to the south and east you can see evidence of reave or boundary systems.

The Deserted Medieval Village

On the north-east facing slope below Hound Tor are the remains of a deserted medieval village, where the remains of the walls of longhouses, barns and outbuildings can be seen.

In 1994, the Dartmoor National Park Authority requested a survey of the settlement area by the Royal Commission on the Historical Monuments of England. The survey discovered that the settlement included four longhouses, four other buildings and three barns with grain dryers. The largest longhouse would have been the Manor House, where the Lord of the Manor lived. He had two gardens attached to his house, a paddock, a cott and a barn.

Not many household artefacts were discovered, only some shards of pottery – pounders, pestles, rubbing stones and whetstones. Nothing that would have been of value was found, which suggests that the occupants took their valuable items with them when they left, so did not leave in a rush.

Life at Hound Tor Village

It is easy to imagine the community out here, in this wonderfully atmospheric place. The villagers would have kept livestock, which they used for meat and milk, and they clearly grew cereal using the field systems, probably using the cattle to pull the ploughs. The corn driers indicate that they grew corn and oats on the land. In the gardens, they would have grown vegetables and

'Medieval Ruins on Hound Tor.' (Miles Wolstenholme)

herbs and maybe kept chickens. From the size of the houses, it looks like there was a cross section of people living here, from domestic servants and land workers to the Lord of the Manor.

It appears that the village was deserted by the middle of the fourteenth century; the reasons for this can only be surmised. We know that the weather changed dramatically during the thirteenth and fourteenth centuries and the climate on the moors became wetter and colder, making it harder to produce enough to eat. The corn, which usually would have been left outdoors to dry in the sun for ten to fourteen days after cutting, was apparently brought inside – judging by the three drying barns. It would have been harder to dry the oats in a wetter climate, and they need to be completely dry before they are taken inside or else they ferment. Also, the animals would have become ill more often in these conditions.

As life was becoming tougher, the Black Death struck in 1348 and roughly one third of the population of Devon died. It can be assumed that Hound Tor village was affected, and this would have been a contributing factor to people abandoning the settlement.

Beech (*Fagus sylvatica*)

Growing in the wooded valleys around the edges of the moors, the beech was also planted as a windbreak on, or near, a stone wall. A tall tree, its leaves create a thick canopy overhead as they align themselves to get as much light as they can. This means that not much rain or light gets through to the forest floor – so not much else grows in beech woodland. Bluebells and wood anemones bloom early in spring, before the beech leaves have opened, and fungi grows well here.

In spring, the soft green leaves of the beech emerge and warm sunlight filters through the new canopy, heralding its arrival. In autumn, the leaves turn a fiery orange and red.

Easdon Down
Lying to the west, and in between North Bovey and Manaton, is a huge mound of land known as Easdon Down. It was clearly a farmed area in prehistoric times, as the edges of the down are covered with the patterns of prehistoric field systems where several reave systems converge around the base. Easdon Down also has the remains of a few hut circles scattered about. These hut circles are wider in diameter (at 7m) than usual hut circles, and it is thought that four adults would have lived in these with their children.

On top of the hill is an ancient cairn with a stone slab in the middle, probably the capstone from a burial kistvaen. It appears that the cairn has been rifled by raiders, who removed stones of sacred burial chambers in search of buried treasure.

The Great Wheal Eleanor
On the north side is the site of an old tin mine, The Great Wheal Eleanor. It is thought that the first mine was opened here between the fifteenth and seventeenth centuries. In 1874, The Great Wheal Eleanor Tin Mining Company was formed to reopen the mines. The mines provided an important source of income and employment for the village of North Bovey. In 1876, it output around 10 tons of black tin and in 1880 it was employing fifteen people from North Bovey. Its success didn't last though, and by 1884 the mine was closed and all the buildings deserted.

The Whooping Rock
Just above Easdon Tor is a logan stone which was named the Whooping Rock because of the noise it made when set in motion by the wind. It was said that in stormy weather, it was heard as far away as 3 miles. A few years ago it was moved off-balance, so it stopped rocking. It was a druidical logan stone and has often been considered an enchanted rock. Whoever moved it from its original position is said to have violated the spirit of the rock.

LUSTLEIGH
A popular and pretty Dartmoor village, full of cosy thatched cottages, Lustleigh is a Dartmoor visitor's friend. It has a full-to-the-brim village shop, a friendly tea room, an old pub and a beautiful orchard, perfect for picnics. In spring, the orchard and the surrounding footpaths and woods come alive with wild flowers, and the villagers prepare to celebrate May Day with one of the most well-known fairs in Devon.

May Day in Lustleigh
On the first Saturday of May, the May Queen leads the procession of maypole dancers through the village under cover of a beautiful canopy of flowers. She is crowned on the May Day Rock in the orchard, and then watches the maypole dancing and other celebrations. Morris dancers perform, a brass band plays, and games and cream teas are enjoyed.

The Beginnings of May Day
The May Day festival dates back to Roman times when the Festival of Flora, the Goddess of fruit and flowers, was celebrated to mark the beginning of summer. It was the custom for everybody to go 'a-Maying' before sunrise on May Day, and to gather flowers and greenery to decorate the village and their homes. Girls would wash their faces in the early morning dew as they believed this would make them beautiful for the coming year. During the day there would be maypole dancing, morris dancing, archery and exhibitions of strength. The highlight of May Day was crowning the May Queen.

The Church

The fact that the oval graveyard around the church is raised above the surrounding village indicates that it was originally an ancient graveyard, dating back to perhaps AD 400.

The church that stands in Lustleigh today was built between 1180 and 1280, but evidence of previous styles of architecture suggest that a former church was originally built before AD 1000, in a Saxon style. The Normans then destroyed the church and would have replaced it with a more substantial and decorative church. This was again knocked down and rebuilt in the Early English and Decorative Style, which is what it is today.

The Old Vestry

This is a granite building in the corner of the churchyard where the Revd William Davy constructed his own printing press and, with the help of his servant, printed his *System of Divinity* in twenty-six volumes.

The Church House

Before the end of the fourteenth century, indoor village activities such as markets, plays, parties and fund raising were held in the nave of village churches. Soon, though, these activities were stopped, as attitudes changed and churches were to be used for religious purposes only. Church Houses were subsequently built for these other activities.

The Old School House

Built in 1876 as a boarding school for eighty children, the Old School House is now a private residence, but you can see the old school bell in the former playground.

Lustleigh. (Author's collection)

The Railway Station

On the line from Moretonhampstead to Newton Abbot (opened in 1866), this railway station was noted for its well-kept garden and its station cat called Jumbo. The line closed to passengers in 1959 and freight in 1964. The station is now a private house.

Lustleigh Cleave

Cleave is the local word for valley. Lustleigh Cleave is the valley through which the River Bovey flows on its way to meet the River Teign. The Cleave is a popular place to walk, with its stunning views.

Red Campion (*Silene dioica*)

You will see this pretty pink flower growing beside the roads in hedgerows around most of the lower lands of Dartmoor. It has a scentless flower unlike campion, the white version, which has a faint scent at night. They grow side-by-side and often fertilise, creating pale pink hybrids.

BOVEY TRACEY

Bovey Tracey, 'Buvvy' in local dialect, is another 'Gateway to the Moors'. A small town situated just off the A38 right on the edge of the moors, with a busy community, an array of interesting shops and plenty of things to see and do.

Its name originates from Saxon times: the first part from the River Bovey, the second from the De Tracey family, who were the Lords of the Manor after the Norman Conquest. William De Tracey was implicated in the murder of the Archbishop Thomas Becket in Canterbury Cathedral in 1170. It is said that he had to rebuild the Church of St Peter, St Paul and St Thomas of Canterbury as penance for the murder.

The church still stands today on the site of the original church, which was built of mud and wattle between AD 400 and 500. Next to the church today you will see a thatched building, 'Church Steps'. This was built in 1490 for use by the church. The uses included meetings, meals and ale brewing. The cross in the graveyard has been rebuilt and uses part of the shaft and one arm of an earlier cross.

A couple of interesting historical events took place in Bovey Tracey in 1646 during the English Civil War. Some Royalist troops were drinking in a local inn when they were attacked by Cromwell's army. Apparently, they escaped the attack by throwing money out of the pub windows. The poorly-paid Roundhead troops were distracted from their attack as they ran to collect the money. However, the next day on Bovey Heath there was another battle between the troops and this time Cromwell's Roundheads won. Signs of the victory are still evident in Bovey Tracey today. The local pub is called the Cromwell's Arms, and a stone arch (the remains of a priory which once stood here) has been named 'Cromwell's Arch'.

At Challacombe Farm, by the footpath into town, stands an old stone cross; this was used as a gatepost. The inscription on a metal plate, dated 1923, claims that the cross had marked the grave of a Royalist officer who fell in 1645.

Bovey Railway Station

At the bottom of town you will find the old railway station. Opened in 1866, the railway was a busy passenger route until 1959 when it was closed to passengers. A goods train ran until 1970. Part of the line is now a road bypass, and part of it diverts off and becomes a woodland walk through the Parke Estate. The station building is now used by the Bovey Tracey Heritage Centre and the goods shed is now used as a store by the Dartmoor National Park Authority.

Bovey Tracey. (Author's collection)

The Devon Guild of Craftsmen

Occupying the Riverside Mill, next to the stone bridge, is the Devon Guild of Craftsmen. It is one of the UK's most acclaimed exhibitions and retail spaces for contemporary craft, founded in 1955 by a group of local people who wished to promote the best in local craftwork. Now it is a leading national educational charity with the aim of creating as many new opportunities as possible for people to enjoy and learn about contemporary craft. At the mill there are always wonderful exhibitions to see, a retail area filled with stunning works to buy and upstairs is a café.

'Guild' traditionally means a community of tradespeople offering mutual support and networking. Today there are 250 members of the Guild who are invited to exhibit and sell their work at the Mill.

The Contemporary Craft Fair

Every year, the Guild hosts the Contemporary Craft Fair in Bovey Tracey – an outdoor fair bringing together over 100 craftsmen to display their wares and run workshops and talks. It is a three-day event crammed with crafts to buy, craft-making workshops, children's craft activities, entertainment and live music, and food and drink.

The Farmers' Market

One of the busiest days to visit Bovey Tracey is when the farmers' market is on. Every two weeks, Union Square is filled with stalls piled high with delicious goods, such as fresh beef, pork and lamb, fresh bread and cakes, cheeses, local vegetables and refreshments.

Parke House

On the outskirts of the town, heading towards Hay Tor Rocks, is Parke House. This is now a National Trust property and is leased to the Dartmoor National Park Authority, who use it as their headquarters. Originally on the site stood a fortified Manor House, and traces of this are visible in the lawn of the present house. The current house was built in the nineteenth century and, although the actual house isn't open to the public, the walled garden with its unusual wall formation (currently under restoration) can be seen. There is an orchard with 150 historic Devon cider-apple trees, a medieval weir on the River Bovey that feeds a fishpond and mill in Bovey Tracey, and various woodland and riverside walks.

Trendlebere Down

In 1997, Trendlebere Down, one of Europe's most important areas of heathland, was destroyed by fire. The flames, which were stopped on the edge of Yarner Wood near Bovey Tracey, engulfed the 300 acres of heathland and all the creatures living there.

The Down, a National Nature Reserve, is managed by English Nature and, after the fire, they launched a five-year management plan to restore the area. The plan has been successful and the heather is back, along with habitats which were destroyed. The gorse has returned and nightjars, linnets, stonechats and skylarks have returned.

Silver Birch (*Betula pendula*)

Native to the UK, the silver birch is recognised by its tall, straight, silvery-white trunk and, although it looks delicate, it is in fact one of the toughest trees in the world. Like the rowan, it likes to grow in high places. This tree was worshipped by the pagan Celtic tribes and was thought to have sacred powers of renewal and purification. Its twigs were used to drive out spirits of the old year, and insane people were 'birched' to expel the evil spirit.

Although the tree doesn't grow large enough in the UK to be used commercially, the wood of the silver birch is used for the backs of brushes and tool handles, and birch twigs are used to make besom brooms for gardens and forest fire beaters.

Ilsington Parish

Ilsington parish is one of the largest in Devon and includes the villages of Ilsington, Haytor Vale, Liverton and South Knighton, plus some interesting parts of the moors. The name is derived from the Domesday name 'Ilestintona'.

The prehistoric reaves which form much of the parish boundary can still be seen. It is amazing to think that the boundary hasn't changed for 4,000 years and many boundary stones still mark the parish boundary. A particularly interesting set of boundary stones erected in the 1850s can be found on Haytor Down. On the back of one stone 'DS' is engraved, probably standing for the Duke of Somerset, who leased parts of the Downs to the Templar family to develop the granite industry. One new stone was unveiled by the Prince of Wales to celebrate the Millennium.

Haytor Rocks

Haytor Rocks is probably the most visited and most photographed tor on Dartmoor. All of the coach tours stop here; there are a couple of large car parks, an information centre and a couple of ice cream vans. It is the hot spot of Dartmoor, probably because it lies next to the road and is easy to walk to; over the years, wide tracks up to the tor have been eroded by the thousands of visitors.

Haytor Rocks is classified as an 'avenue tor'; there are two massive granite outcrops, the central section having been eroded to leave an avenue between them. The tor is 1495ft (457m) high.

'Melting Snow at Haytor Rocks.' (Mike Bartholomew)

'Haytor Granite Tramway.' (Miles Wolstenholme)

On the eastern outcrop is a rock basin, which you can climb up relatively easily as some steps were cut into the granite back in the 1800s. There was also an iron handrail built; Hemery, in 1983, noted an interesting remark made by a Doctor Coker in 1851: '...the unsightly stair step to enable the enervated and pinguedinous scions of humanity of this wonderful nineteenth century to gain the summit.' Today the tor is popular with climbers.

Emperor Moth (*Saturnia pavonia*)

This moth has pretty distinctive wings, with large eye-spots on all four of them. It is found on heaths, moors and marshes. Its caterpillar spins a silk cocoon which is large and rough – and commercially worthless. This brown, pear-shaped cocoon has a ring of spines at the sharp end, which open when pressed from the inside by the moth who wants to emerge, but cannot be opened from the outside.

Granite Quarries

There are two quarries in the area, Holwell Quarry and Haytor Quarry. Both were in use in the 1800s–1900s. Granite was taken from Haytor Quarry (which can be found north of Haytor Rocks) and used to build London Bridge and The British Museum. The quarry is now flooded and nature has claimed it back from its industrial past, making it a home for dragonflies, frogs, water lilies and goldfish – although an old winch and parts of a derrick can still be seen. The last stone to be extracted was in 1919, for the Exeter War Memorial.

On the south-east side of Haytor Quarry is the site of the original Haytor village, consisting of quarry workers' cottages. The village was abandoned around 1860 with the decline in quarrying, and the workers moved down to the new cottages at Haytor Vale. Today, all that can be seen is a gatepost, a few trees and the outlines of the buildings.

Just below the tramway, near Holwell Quarry, is a workmen's hut with its roof constructed from two granite slabs. It may have been used as a store for tools, or as a shelter from blasting.

The Granite Tramway

In 1776, George Templar built an 8½-mile tramway from Haytor Quarry to Stover Canal. He had received a contract to supply Haytor granite for the rebuilding of London Bridge, and the old transport method of horse and cart just wasn't good enough. He constructed a tramway to link the quarries to Stover Canal, which had been built earlier by his father to carry ball clay from the Teign Valley. From here, the granite was taken by barge to Teignmouth for shipping.

There is therefore a vast network of tramways on the moor, connecting to the different quarries. The track is clearly visible and in good condition. The length of the rails varies between 4ft and 8ft, and the width is 4ft 3in – not a lot smaller than today's railways. The tramway was last used in the 1850s and is now a recognised walk – the Templar Way.

Bracken (*Pteridium aquilinum*)

Bracken is amongst a family of the coarsest ferns. It is one of the oldest ferns, with fossil records of over 55 million years old having been found. The plant sends up large, triangular fronds from a wide-creeping underground rootstock, and may form dense thickets. It is widespread and abundant on the moors, and takes over grazing areas by replacing the grass and heather.

Red Grouse (*Lagopus lagopus*)

Plump-bodied with a short tail and dark, reddish-brown plumage, this game bird can startle you, squawking and flapping its wings, if it is disturbed on the moors. The mature heather of the moors provides cover for this bird and here it makes its nest, a shallow hollow scarped out by the female. It feeds on the young heather shoots, seeds, berries and insects. The population is declining now, probably due to the disappearance of heath moorland.

ILSINGTON

Ilsington village is believed to be an ancient settlement, existing around 200–300 years before the Norman Conquest. Throughout the years, it seems that Ilsington was mainly self-supporting, and records show a variety of rural occupations among the local inhabitants (farmers, butchers, bakers, tailors, miners, millers, weavers, blacksmiths, carpenters, shoemakers, thatchers etc.).

It is known that there was a church there in the eleventh century, on the site of the present church. The present church, St Michael's, dates back to the beginning of the fourteenth century and was extended in the fifteenth century as a result of prosperity from the wool and tin mining industries. It has tinners' rabbits on the roof bosses and, unique to Devon, the clergy stall is made from medieval poppy-head bench ends. In a corner of the churchyard, you can see the remains of the ancient Manor House which fell into ruin after the occupation ended in about 1825.

The west lychgate (a gateway covered with a roof, normally at the entrance to a churchyard), was once a school. That was until Tuesday, 17 September 1639, when a woman slammed the heavy oak door and the whole building collapsed. Four boys fell into the graveyard, one onto the street and the rest were covered in rubble. Luckily, none of them were seriously injured. In 1910, the building was rebuilt to a design by T.H. Lyon, the well-known architect.

One problem Ilsington had was that it didn't have a spring for water. There was a leat running from Haytor but it was often polluted. So, villagers who didn't have their own wells would either collect water from a spring in a field on the way to Simms Hill, or from the brook at Narrowcombe. Fortunately, a piped water supply was installed in 1914 from a new reservoir near the Haytor Quarries.

Today there is a pub in Ilsington called the Carpenters Arms. It is thought that it used to be a farmhouse before becoming a pub in 1816. There is also a hotel, the Ilsington Country House Hotel, which offers holiday accommodation and conference facilities.

HAYTOR VALE

Haytor Vale was a small holding of Smallacombe Farm, known as Kennapark Wells until the early nineteenth century. George Templar, who was building the granite tramway to Stover, had a row of cottages built here to house the quarry workers. The Rock Inn was built at the same time. In 1900, several more houses were built, designed by the local architect T.H. Lyon.

LIVERTON

Believing that the London to Penzance railway line was going to be passing through Liverton, Henry Beare, an agricultural engineer, built a foundry at Liverton. When he realised his mistake, he moved his business to Newton Abbot. A pottery took over the Liverton site and became the Devonmoor Art Pottery, employing forty people until it closed in the 1950s. In 2002, the site was converted into a housing development known as Potters Yard. The village has a traditional country pub, the Star Inn.

'Sunset Near Saddle Tor.' (Mike Bartholomew)

Trumpeter

A small village in the parish of Ilsington which derived its name from 'Tromptsmede' – which means 'the meadow of one called Trump'. The area was a tin and copper mining area and the Atlas Tin Mining Co., which operated many of the mines, was based in Trumpeter. Along the track to Smallacombe Farm was the entrance to one large mine, whilst in the opposite direction, up the lane to Lowthorne Cross, was the Atlas Mine. The burning house, which was built with stone from the quarries, was on the right-hand side of the lane towards Middlecott. This mine was worked from the 1850s until 1903.

Mining in the area

There were many tin mines in the Ilsington parish and much evidence can still be seen, particularly on the open moorland from Hemsworthy Gate to Bagtor. These were known as the Haytor Consoles and were worked from 1854. The steam engine used to be fired by peat!

Opposite Bagtor, on the slopes of Pinchford Ball, you can see an extensive area of workings known as Bagtor Mine or Crowley Park Mine. These were worked from 1845 to 1867. Further down, the Smiths Wood and Sigford Consoles were worked from 1819 to 1863 for both tin and copper.

Saddle Tor

This is another popular tor to visit and photograph. You will see it on the right as you drive past Haytor Rocks towards Widecombe.

Bilberry (*Vaccinium myrtillus*)

Also known as the whortleberry, this bush grows on the high heaths of the moors, liking the poor soils. In spring it has drooping pink flowers, and in the autumn its black berries are wonderful food for grouse and other birds.

The bilberry can be eaten raw, with cream, or made into pies and jellies. It is rich in Vitamin C and D, and in the Middle Ages was a remedy for diarrhoea and dysentery. In Scotland, bilberry juice was used to make a purple dye for paper, linens and wool.

Rippon Tor

A much more interesting, but less visited, tor is Rippon Tor. It was recorded originally as being called Rippentor, but nobody seems to know the origin of the name. Rippon Tor is 473m high and there are some stunning views from its peak.

For centuries it has been used as a landmark by sailors coming into Teignmouth and Dartmouth, as it is so prominent. The tor consists of several rock piles and there are the remains of three cairns on its summit. The cairn on the highest pile is supposedly the largest cairn on Dartmoor, with its diameter of 28m and height of 4m. There is a trig point in the middle of this cairn. Rippon Tor is the eighth highest tor on Dartmoor.

Rippon Tor also boasts having the largest reave or boundary system in Britain. There are signs of two parallel reaves on the tor, which form part of the whole system of between 3,300 and 4,500 hectares. A connecting cross bank, which seems to separate the cairns from the field system, suggests that prehistoric man wanted to keep the sacred rituals separate from the farming. There are a few hut circles around the tor, which interestingly don't appear to be connected to the field system so were perhaps used for storage or for temporary shelter, such as shepherds' huts.

Another historical find on Rippon Tor is the Latin Cross which is lying buried in the turf about 20m from the trig point. The cross was clearly being cut *in situ* but is unfinished, and there is some dispute as to what it was for. Some believe that it wasn't actually ever meant to be erected and was cut here in order to 'Christianise' the Bronze Age or pagan burial cairns.

To the south-west of the tor is the logan stone known as the 'Nutcrackers'. This is supposedly Dartmoor's largest logan stone.

'Rippon Tor.' (Mike Bartholomew)

A Haunting. Newhouse Inn, Hemsworthy Gate

If you happen to be travelling along the road between Hemsworthy Gate and Cold East Cross on a moonlit night, keep your eyes peeled for the headless horseman. He has been described as wearing an old-fashioned military coat, and the stories say that this spectral figure slows down as it passes the ruined Newhouse Inn, and then gathers speed once again.

Who was this horseman and where was he going? Nobody really knows, but this road used to be a busy track across the moors, linking Ashburton with Chagford, Bovey Tracey and Moretonhampstead. The Newhouse Inn was obviously a much-welcomed watering hole for travellers. Was he a highwayman who frequented the neighbourhood? Could it be that he was a lost traveller, sucked into the swamps of Blackslade Mire? Did the marsh lights lure him to his death?

The remains of the Newhouse Inn can be seen at Hemsworthy, by the side of the road towards Cold East Cross. The building burnt down 150 years ago in mysterious circumstances, and now it takes a while to distinguish the remains amongst the surrounding rocks. Was the spectral figure something to do with the burning?

Adding to the eerie reputation, the moorland around this stretch of road is littered with many prehistoric sites. On the slopes above is a reave system, Foales Arrishes (see p.62), and various Bronze Age hut circles, and near the road is an ancient prehistoric barrow, The Seven Lords. Blackslade Mire is also close by.

WIDECOMBE IN THE MOOR

Cradled in the hollow of the East Webburn Valley, in the middle of the desolate moor, Widecombe is the best-known and most commercialised village on Dartmoor. Renowned around the world for its folk song 'Old Uncle Tom Cobley and All', and around Devon for the annual Widecombe Fair, Widecombe is in fact only a small village of around 200 inhabitants. Its distinctive and majestic church tower can be seen for miles around. Widecombe has many beautiful buildings and places of interest, and is a very welcoming place to visit after travelling across the open moors.

Fact or Fiction?

The church, sometimes known as 'the cathedral of the moor' due to its high tower (120ft), is dedicated to St Pancras. Inside the south-side entrance to the church, on the wall, you can read about the fateful evening of Sunday, 21 October 1638, when the church was shaken by a terrible thunderstorm and the pinnacle of the tower came crashing through the roof, killing one man and injuring many others. Legend has it that the Devil came to Widecombe to collect the souls of those playing cards at the rear of the church. He called at the Tavistock Inn in Poundsgate to enquire the way, paying for his drink with money that later turned into a dead beech leaf. When he reached the church, he tied his horse to the pinnacle of the tower, gathered up the gamblers and swept them away. However, he forgot to untie his horse and, as he rode off, the pinnacle broke and came crashing through the roof.

The Church House

The Church House is the large granite building in the centre of the village, built around 1500 near the old yew tree. It was probably built by the masons, who built the church tower, and was originally a resting place for travellers, a workshop, alehouse, almshouses and later, the village school. It is now owned by The National Trust and used as the village hall.

Under the covered walkway you will see an old naval shell, donated to the village after the First World War as a thank you to the villagers who collected sphagnum moss from the surrounding bogs for use as emergency field dressings.

Widecombe in the Moor. (Author's collection)

Widecombe church. (Author's collection)

The Old Inn

This large and cosy pub was built during the fourteenth century. It was severely damaged in 1977 by a fire, but has been beautifully restored whilst still retaining its old character. It is now a very popular place to eat and has a wonderful, friendly atmosphere, so is worth a visit if you are in Widecombe.

The Village Sign

On the grass verge in front of the church is a carved granite sign with a carving of Old Uncle Tom Cobley. This was put here in 1948. The original sign was made of coloured tiles and stood on the village green, but was taken down during the Second World War, when all village signs had to be removed.

Widecombe Fair

Widecombe Fair used to take place every year on the village green. It started as a fair where the local farmers would sell their stock, buy fresh breeding stock and exchange their bulls, rams and stallions. It took place in autumn and was one of the main trading days in the year for local farmers.

Today it takes place on a permanent site opposite the school, on the second Tuesday in September. It is no longer an animal-trading fair but a fair for all, attracting thousands of visitors each year. There are classes for rural produce, craft stalls, sheepdog demonstrations, ponies and sheep are displayed, there are vintage tractors, a gymkhana, fancy-dress, a tug o' war, bale tossing, dancing and a barbeque. And 'Old Uncle Tom Cobley' rides around the village on his Old Grey Mare, re-enacting the folk song.

Sphagnum Moss

Sphagnum moss is a peat moss which grows in bogs and mires. It is extremely absorbent and acidic, and inhibits the growth of bacteria and fungi. It has been used for centuries as a dressing for wounds and, during the First World War, the villagers of Widecombe collected the moss for use in emergency field dressings.

Tunhill or Blackslade Kistvaen

Out on Blackslade Down you can see the four remaining granite slabs of a Bronze Age tomb, where the cremated remains of a warrior were buried.

Foales Arrishes

Foales Arrishes is the remains of a Bronze Age reave system lying between Blackslade Down and Top Tor. The low banks of earth and stone, running parallel to each other, formed straight and regular patterns which probably contained fields. It is thought that Foales Arrishes may have been occupied during the Iron Age, which is unusual for Dartmoor.

The Giant's Chair

Unfortunately, you won't be able to see this interesting Dartmoor feature any longer as it has gone. It was a huge 20ft (6m) wooden chair erected by an artist on private land, an extraordinary and inspiring work of art that people flocked to see. However, the owner was only granted temporary retrospective planning permission.

The chair was a victim of its own success, as the local roads got jammed with the traffic of people wanting a glimpse and, although the Dartmoor National Park Authority expressed its support for the project, it was agreed that it wasn't in the appropriate location.

In July 2010, it was dismantled and is being stored whilst the artist seeks a new home for it. A campaign on social networking site Facebook, called 'Save the Giant's Chair', attracted more than 6,000 members.

Hamel Down (or Hameldon Ridge)

Hamel Down is a huge, rounded ridge, crossed by the Two Moors Way. The top of the ridge can be reached by a climb from Grimspound at the northern end, or from the Widecombe area at the southern end. The views from its heights are spectacular and well worth the climb, and there are plenty of prehistoric remnants around to add interest to a walk along the ridge.

Hameldown Beacon

This site is recorded as being one of the many sites on Dartmoor where beacon fires were lit in an emergency. Hameldown Beacon was in a chain with Buckland Beacon to the SSE and Meldon Hill to the NNW. Between the beacons, the signal reached 8½ miles.

In the past, the quickest way to communicate an emergency was to climb to a high point and light a fire. As there are so many high points on Dartmoor, it became the place to send out signals in all directions.

There were various types of beacon, from a stone-built turret to an iron basket, sometimes referred to as a cresset, placed on top of a pole. In daylight, smoke would be used for signalling, whereas during the night a flaming fire would be used. Most of the beacons were sited on the top of hills, but in some cases an ecclesiastical site would have been used. Most beacon sites seem to be located at sites previously used by prehistoric man, as they both needed high vantage points. Examples include Brentor, Cosdon, Eastern Beacon, Hameldown, North Hessary Tor, Penn Beacon, Prestonbury Camp, Western Beacon and Yes Tor. Here there are either Bronze Age

'The Giant's Chair, Natsworthy.' (Mike Bartholomew)

cairns or Iron Age settlements. Hameldown Beacon was also used in later years as the site of a boundary stone for Natsworthy Manor.

Hameldown Cross

A rather worn-looking one-armed cross can be found just off the main track. Although not a wonderful example of a well-carved cross, it is the highest cross on Dartmoor at 524m. Experts agree that it was moved from its original spot to where it is now to be used as a boundary stone, marking the limits of Natsworthy Manor. When moved, it was marked with the boundary markings 'HC' for Hameldown Cross and 'DS' for Duke of Somerset and the year 1854. The 11th Duke of Somerset bought Natsworthy Manor in 1854. The cross dates back to medieval times and it isn't known why it would be up here amongst the barrows and cairns of the pagan burial grounds.

Two Barrows

Further along the Two Moors way, heading towards Grimspound, you will come across Two Barrows – which consists of two barrows lying to the side of the track about 4m apart. The northern barrow was excavated in 1872 and a lump of charcoal was discovered in the central cairn. To the south-east of the central cairn they found a mass of bones covered by five flat slabs of stone. Amongst the bones was a precious dagger pommel, carved out of amber and studded with gold pins. This was dated back to 1500 BC. Half a metre away, the bronze dagger blade was found. It was clear that whoever was buried in this barrow was someone important, such as a tribal leader. The dagger was kept in Plymouth museum until the building was destroyed in one of Hitler's bombing raids.

In between the two barrows is what is known as a Duke Stone, one of the stones erected in the nineteenth century by the Duke of Somerset as a boundary mark.

Single Barrow

A little way off is a single cairn known as the Single Barrow. When this was excavated in 1873 all that was found was a pile of cremated bones, some charcoal and a flint flake. This cairn also contains a 'DS' boundary stone, carved with the words 'Single Barrow'.

Broad Barrow

Further on there is yet another barrow, Broad Barrow, right in the middle of the track. This is also marked with a 'DS' stone, this time saying 'Broad Barrow'.

Hameldown Tor (also known as Hameldon Tor)

Hameldown Tor stands 529m above sea level, with amazing views over to Cosdon Hill in the north and Rippon Tor to the south-east. It is on the path of the Two Moors Way as it crosses Hamel Down.

Hameldown Tor is one of the many aircraft crash sites on Dartmoor. There were many airfields in Devon during the war and many planes coming in to land crashed on the moors. The crash that happened here occurred on 21 March 1941. A Hampden, belonging to the 49 squadron of 5 group bomber command, was returning to RAF Scampton, in Lincolnshire, after an operation and crashed into the tor because of the bad visibility. A memorial was cut into the granite boulder on the tor.

There is a story that, on 21 March 1971, some walkers were coming up over Hameldown Tor in the late evening when one of them, a visitor to the area, suddenly threw himself on the ground with his hands over his head. He said he saw what looked like a twin bomber flying directly towards him. Nobody else saw anything but he was absolutely convinced. It was around 11 p.m., roughly the time of the crash thirty years ago.

1 'Black a Tor Copse.' (Miles Wolstenholme)

2 'Windy Post, Dartmoor.' (Miles Wolstenholme)

3 'Scorhill Clapper.' (Miles Wolstenholme)

4 'Sunset at Top Tor.' (Mike Bartholomew)

5 'Let's stick together.' (Miles Wolstenholme)

7 'Haytor Rocks.' (Mike Bartholomew)

6 'Sun over Widecombe in the Moor.' (Mike Bartholomew)

8 'Dartmoor Through the Mist.' (Miles Wolstenholme)

9 'Autumn Fungi.' (Mike Bartholomew)

10 'Evening Glow on Prewley Moor, Dartmoor.' (Miles Wolstenholme)

11 'Fungi.'
(Mike Bartholomew)

12 'Sunset at
Fenworthy
Reservoir.' (Mike
Bartholomew)

13 'Foggintor Quarry, Dartmoor.' (Miles Wolstenholme)

14 'Lesser Celandine.' (Mike Bartholomew)

15 'Grimpsound Enclosure, Dartmoor.' (Miles Wolstenholme)

16 'Sunset over Brentor.' (Miles Wolstenholme)

17 'Tree at Coombestone Tor.' (Mike Bartholomew)

18 'Silver-Washed Fritillary.' (Miles Wolstenholme)

19 'Wheal Betsy
Engine House.'
(Miles Wolstenholme)

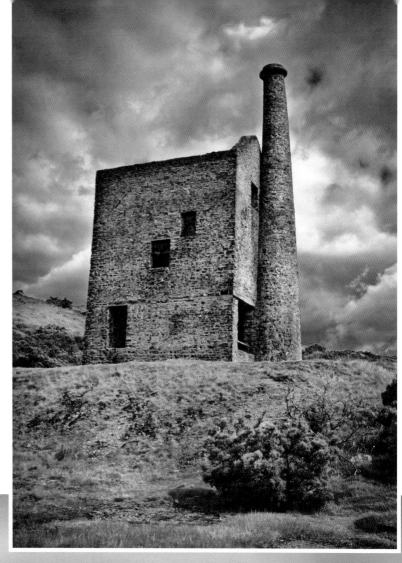

20 'Bluebells.'
(Mike Bartholomew)

21 'Dartmoor Ponies.' (Mike Bartholomew)

22 'Windswept Tree Near Saddle Tor.' (Mike Bartholomew)

23 'The Nine Maidens Circle, Belstone.' (Mike Bartholomew)

24 'Reflections at Fernworthy.' (Mike Bartholomew)

25 'Waterfall on East Okement.' (Miles Wolstenholme)

26 'A Flock of Golden Plovers Fly Past Haytor Rocks.' (Mike Bartholomew)

27 'Sheep at Sunset.' (Mike Bartholomew)

28 'Storm Clouds on Belstone Common.' (Mike Bartholomew)

29 'Time for a Drink.' (Miles Wolstenholme)

30 'Puddles at Coombestone Tor.' (Mike Bartholomew)

Common Heath or Ling (*Calluna vulgaris*)

This heather is dominant on heath and moorland locations, and on Dartmoor it carpets some areas during the summer. It is tolerant of grazing and will regenerate after burning. It is eaten by deer and sheep, and red grouse feed on the young shoots and seeds.

The Meadow Pipit (*Anthus pratensis*)

A small, brown streaked bird with white outer tail feathers, the meadow pipit breeds on the open moorland and can often be seen and heard during its song flight. It climbs up to 100ft (30m) with its series of fast chirps, which slow down as it reaches its peak, and then it slowly drops down with outspread, upward-pointing wings and tail, to land with a final trill.

It builds its nest amongst the grasses at the edges of meadows and usually lays three to five eggs, which sometimes harbour a cuckoo's egg.

PONSWORTHY

Ponsworthy is a pretty hamlet in the valley of the West Webburn River, around 3½ miles from Widecombe. The picturesque cottages running down the hill are often seen on postcards, and there is an old mill and an old bakehouse, which has been converted to a house. Ponsworthy House is notable for its wonderful porch, constructed with Doric columns of granite (a feature of classical Greek architecture).

The village has a very narrow bridge over the river which, according to the engraved dates on the stone, dates back to 1666. The other date, 1792, is believed to be when repairs were carried out. One of the reasons the village is so quiet is because the bridge is only 7½ft wide (2.3m), making it too narrow for the tourist coaches.

West Webburn River

This pretty river begins on the hills near Cator Common and flows down the east side through Shallowford, and on to pass through Ponsworthy where it is crossed by the road at what is called the 'Ponsworthy Splash'. It joins the East Webburn River, which begins its life on Hamel Down at Lizwell, and together they flow through the wooded valley to meet the River Dart.

POUNDSGATE

On the road from Ashburton to Two Bridges you will pass through Poundsgate, a small village consisting of a few cottages, some farms and a pub dating back to the thirteenth century. The Tavistock Inn is a cosy old pub and very popular with tourists as it is right on the main road. Poundsgate derived its name from the pound just outside the village on the left-hand side of the road. It used to have its own post office, garage and shop, but these have closed down in recent years.

Poundsgate has its own Wesleyan Chapel, built in the eighteenth century when the Wesleyan movement hit the West Country. It is easily spotted, being on the main road, and services are held here on the first Sunday of every month.

BUCKLAND IN THE MOOR

Another pretty Dartmoor village filled with thatched cottages, the main attraction of Buckland in the Moor is its church, St Peter's. It is famous for its unusual clock face and attracts hundreds of visitors. The clock and three new bells were donated to the church in 1930 by the Lord of the Manor, William Whitely, but, instead of numbers being written on the clock face, he had inscribed 'My Dear Mother', as a tribute to his parent. The clock was made by John Smith & Sons of Derby, who were reputed for their clocks and chiming bells. Examples of their work can be seen in St Paul's Cathedral.

It is thought that the original church was built on this site during the twelfth century, and there are plenty of interesting features to be seen here. As you walk into the churchyard, you will see a group of 'Dartmoor' headstones. This is where the Whitely family are buried. On each

Cottages at Ponsworthy. (Author's collection)

The Tavistock Inn, Poundsgate. (Author's collection)

'St Peter's Church, Buckland in the Moor.' (Miles Wolstenholme)

gravestone is the inscription 'Live to Live'. At the bottom of the churchyard is an old thatched vestry, probably the only thatched vestry still in use in the UK and one of only four thatched buildings on Dartmoor that are used for work purposes, not as a house.

Taking the path towards the gateway from the vestry, you can see the remains of what is thought to be an old wayside cross. The base of the cross is said to be the huge pedestal which stands outside the churchyard and now has a tree in it.

Buckland Beacon

Standing at 382m, Buckland Beacon offers some stunning panoramic views of the deep-wooded valleys of the River Dart. As the name indicates, its high point was one of the fire beacon sites of Dartmoor. An inscription on a rock reads:

> Buckland Beacon. A beacon fire one of a chain lit here by the parishioners of Buckland in the Moor in celebration of their Majesties silver jubilee May 6th 1935. and the people shouted and said 'God save the King'.

The beacon was also part of the fire chain of beacons used for the Millennium celebrations and Queen Elizabeth's Jubilee celebrations.

The Ten Commandments stone

In 1928, a proposed new Book of Common Prayer was rejected by Parliament, which was considered by many to be a victory for the Protestants. In celebration of this victory, Mr William Whitely, the Lord of the Manor, commissioned W. A. Clement, a sculptor from Exmouth, to engrave two granite slabs on Buckland Beacon with the Ten Commandments.

Whilst he worked on the commandments, Mr Clement lived in a cowshed on the edge of the nearby woods, with some wire netting for a bed and the stream nearby to wash in and drink from. He worked nine and a half hours a day, cutting 1,547 letters into the stone for the price of £50. He started work on 23 July and finished on 31 August 1928. He was nicknamed 'Moses'.

Four commandments are written on one of the slabs, along with a favourite quotation of Mr Whitely. On the other slab, the remaining six commandments are engraved, along with an extra one used to fill in the gap. This reads:

> A new commandment I give unto you. Love one another.
>
> *John, Chapter 13, Verse 34*

In 1995, the letters were recut and painted black on instructions from the Dartmoor National Park Authority and the current landowner, Mr Whitely.

The Raven

Ravens are relatively common on Dartmoor as they tend to live in unpopulated areas. Disliked by men, they are seen as harbingers of death and live on cliffs, quarries, windswept hills and moorland. Their dark reputation stems from many years ago, when they would feed on the corpses hanging from the gibbet. Their jet black colour and stout, heavy bill add to their gloomy appearance, and their coarse croak resounds over the moorland. They feed on carrion such as small mammals and sometimes dead sheep or lamb, also foraging for eggs, reptiles, insects and seeds. The raven is the largest species of perching bird in the world. They build their nests from twigs, sticks, heather, earth and moss.

ASHBURTON

Ashburton is one of the four stannary towns of Dartmoor, located on the eastern edge of the moors beside the A38. It originally developed in Saxon times, although little is known about this period. Some prehistoric finds were discovered that date back to 3000 BC, but there isn't evidence of a settlement here until 500 BC. The name recorded for Ashburton in the Domesday Book is 'Essebreton'.

Ashburton probably developed here due to the presence of tin, and was designated a stannary town in 1285. The tinners would send their tin ingots here by packhorse and the stannary officials and dealers would gather to examine and buy the tin. Ashburton became the most important stannary town in Devon and, in 1515, about forty per cent of Devon's tin passed through the town. By the early 1700s, the trade had all but died out – but small amounts have been mined even up to comparatively recent times.

Ashburton Museum

The Ashburton Museum is found next door to Lloyds Bank in the centre of town. It originally started life in a private house, but soon outgrew it and moved into the tower of St Lawrence's Chapel. In 1962 the museum moved into the old blacksmith's shop behind the chapel, and then in 1968 it moved again to where it is today – to a building which used to be a brush factory.

It contains a unique collection of local artefacts, plus it houses the internationally known Endacott Collection of North American Indian items. It isn't open every day, so before planning a visit it is worth checking with the information centre for opening times.

Ashburton. (Author's collection)

Historical Buildings of Interest

The Card House

Now a small supermarket, this building was once a gaming house. If you look carefully at the slates on the frontage, you will see they are carved with different suits of cards.

The Mermaid Inn

Ashburton's hardware shop was once the Mermaid Inn, with its medieval arched granite doorway. General Fairfax, the Civil War Roundhead leader, stayed here when the Roundheads fled after their defeat in Bovey Tracey.

The Golden Lion

Built in 1790 for the surgeon Nicholas Tripe, this is now a private house. It was the home of Alan Hope, a publican and the first elected candidate of the Official Monster Raving Loony Party, who later became Mayor of Ashburton.

The United Reform Church

Now an antique fireplace emporium, this building retains many of its old features – including its stained-glass windows.

The Chapel of St Lawrence

This chapel is now a Grade II listed building. It started life as a private chapel built for the Bishop of Exeter in 1301, Bishop Stapledon, who was Lord of the Manor. He dedicated it to St Lawrence; it was built next to his home and is sometimes referred to as his palace.

In 1314 the Bishop gave the chapel to the town, stipulating that a priest be appointed to say prayers for his soul and all the past and future Bishops of Exeter. The Guild of St Lawrence was appointed to manage the chantry and the chapel's affairs. It appears that there was a small school here, run by the priest, which thrived for 600 years.

In 1938, the County Council decided to close the school due to falling numbers, but the building was still used as an annexe to the county and primary schools until the 1980s.

In 1984, the Guild of St Lawrence was reformed to protect and preserve the building which was in danger of collapse through neglect and, in 1986, it was fully restored and is now a Heritage, Cultural and Community Centre run by the Guild of St Lawrence.

The Parish Church of St Andrew

Originally built at the end of the twelfth century, this splendid-looking church was entirely rebuilt in the fifteenth century. Its tower is an amazing 92ft and, like all the Dartmoor churches, it has no spire. Over the west door stand three modern statues tucked into niches. The inside of the church is just as stunning, with its wagon roof and roof bosses.

Nb. A wagon roof is a roof constructed of a closely-spaced series of double arch-braced trusses, giving it the shape of a wagon or barrel vault. On the inside the roof may be exposed, plastered or panelled. A roof boss is an ornamental knob covering the intersection of ribs in a vault or on a ceiling.

Ashburton's Methodist Church

John Wesley, founder of the Methodist Church, declared that Ashburton was 'the most heathen town he had ever visited'. A Church House was established on Woodland Road eventually, which then led to the building of the Ashburton Methodist Church. Today the church is used for playgroups and theatres, as well as worship, weddings and funerals.

Catholic Church of our Lady of Lourdes and St Petroc
When the monks came to Buckfast Abbey in 1882, there were no Catholics in the Ashburton area. It wasn't long, though, before Abbot Boniface decided to revive Catholicism in Ashburton, and in 1911 the first mass took place in a temporary chapel. It was a barn in Roborough Lane. In 1933 the present site on Eastern Road was acquired, and in November 1935 the Church of our Lady of Lourdes and St Petroc was opened.

The Portreeve

Ashburton is one of only six towns today which have a portreeve (port warden). A portreeve is a political appointment dating back to the reign of Edward the Elder, who wanted to ensure that taxes were paid correctly. Under his reign it was forbidden to conduct trade outside of an appointed place of trading (a port) and without the supervision of a portreeve or other trustworthy person. In other words, a portreeve was very much like a revenue and customs officer.

By the late Middle Ages, a portreeve acted as a representative of the people, ensuring their duties to the Mayor and the community were fulfilled. In some cases the role was also that of Mayor. The five other towns in the UK that have portreeves are Laugharne, Beccles, Callington, Cheevel and Yeovil.

Today the portreeve in Ashburton upholds an ancient tradition. Each year in the Chapel of St Lawrence, the portreeve is appointed and sworn in at a ceremony, along with his bailiff, ale tasters, bread weighers and other ancient offices.

Heath Spotted Orchid (*Dactylorhiza maculate*)

This orchid grows on heaths, moors and bogs and is the most common of orchids. It also grows on sphagnum moss in some areas. Lots of insects are attracted to its flower as it produces a sugary liquid in the spur. This is how it pollinates; its stamens stick to parts of the insect's head and the insect then carries the pollen to another flower.

Newbridge

> NEWBRIDGE
> A place where I was ten again,
> Over a tree bridge to an island of adventure
> With moss so green it spoke of magic,
> Smelt of centuries,
> Where the river giggled
> Its mocking song,
> Telling secrets
> I would never decode
>
> *Jennie Osborne*

On the road from Ashburton to Two Bridges, you cross the River Dart. The bridge you travel over was built in 1413 and is constructed from granite. It is a Grade II listed medieval bridge with three semi-circular arches. The two pillars have 'cut waters' which deflect the flow of the water. These extend up to road level, where they provide triangular refuge places for pedestrians to escape the traffic.

The area is very popular with tourists and the large car park over the bridge is always full during summer. Kayakers and canoeists swarm here and it is now a recognised British Canoe Union access point.

Newbridge. (Author's collection)

Goosander (*Mergus merganser*)

The goosander lives on the reservoirs of the moors and nests in holes inside trees, or in holes in the banks amongst boulders. The young bird will often fall a few feet as it leaves the nest, because it departs before it can fly.

During the breeding season you will see the male birds with their stunning dark green heads and pinky-white bodies. The female has a brown head and they both have narrow red bills.

The Coffin Stone

As you near Dartmeet, on the road from Poundsgate, you can see a granite slab lying on the left-hand side of the road. It is the 'coffin stone' and you will recognise it by the initials and crosses carved on its sides.

Years ago, coffins were carried miles across the moors on the shoulders of six of the mourners. The remaining mourners followed behind in two rows. A conductor led the way and every so often would signal to the first six mourners behind, and they would speed up to take the place of the bearers. The bearers could then drop back and rest. In this way, the procession could continue at a regular pace.

However, some of the walks were long and steep, and the procession needed to stop for a rest. The coffin stone was one of the places where they would rest the coffin.

Rumour has it that whilst one particularly nasty person was being carried to his burial, the bearers put the coffin down on this particular stone to rest. Suddenly a bolt of lightning flashed down from the sky with a deep rumble of thunder and hit the stone. As the smoke lifted, it was seen that the coffin had been shattered and the coffin stone was split in two. This explains why some people think the coffin stone is two stones and not one.

The Stonechat (*Saxicola torquata*)

This small bird is a member of the thrush family and derives its name from its call, which sounds like pebbles being knocked together. Found on the heathland on Dartmoor, it can often be seen perched in a low bush flicking its wings. It has a striking black head with a chestnut breast and dark back, with white patches on it neck. The female has a brown head and back, and an orangey breast.

Stonechats eat insects, worms, spiders and seeds. Their nests are built from moss, grass and hair, and are usually hidden low down in thick grass or bushes.

The male has several mates who will lay five or six eggs; he helps to feed the young until they can fly. These birds stay in the UK all year and the female has up to three broods a year, as many of them die during severe winters.

SOUTH DARTMOOR

BUCKFASTLEIGH

Buckfastleigh is an historic mill town just off the A38, on the southern edge of the moors. It is a quiet town with an interesting collection of shops selling second-hand furniture and local arts and crafts.

It is thought that Buckfast existed before Buckfastleigh, as there was mention of it in the Domesday Book. The abbey at Buckfast was built in 1018 and Buckfastleigh probably developed as a settlement of the abbey.

The name Buckfastleigh means 'deer held in a pasture', with Buckfast meaning 'stronghold' and Leigh meaning 'pasture that belongs to Buckfast'. Another interesting point about the name is that it contains half the letters of the alphabet and none of them are repeated.

Buckfastleigh developed where two small streams, the River Mardle and the Dean Burn, converged and flowed into the Dart. This running water made it an ideal location for mills and the town soon developed its woollen industry. In fact, it is well known for its woollen mills, corn and paper mills and a tannery. In the sixteenth century about five mills were working, and in 1850 it was recorded that there were two serge mills (serge being a type of twill fabric with diagonal lines or ridges on both sides, made with a two-up, two-down weave. The worsted variety is used in making military uniforms, suits, great coats and trench coats) and 300 woolcombers. In the nineteenth century, the town reached its industrial peak and many houses were built to house the workers along with many public buildings: the Town Hall, the community hall, Victoria Park, the tennis courts and the swimming pool. The new primary school was built in 1875 and the railway line from Buckfastleigh and Ashburton to Totnes was opened.

Buckfastleigh developed in two parts – Lower Town and Higher Town – Lower Town being built in the late eighteenth to early nineteenth century, while Higher Town was built during the nineteenth century. They were actually two separate settlements until the mid-nineteenth century, and the boys hung around in gangs called the higher towners and the lower towners – with many scraps between them.

The Holy Trinity Church

Originally built in the thirteenth century and then rebuilt in the fifteenth century, this church was destroyed by a fire on 21 July 1992 and is now only a shell with the tower and spire remaining. The bells, which originally came from the abbey, survived the fire and have been rehung. There are some ruins of a thirteenth-century chantry chapel standing to the east in the churchyard but not much is known of its history.

Opposite the porch you will see what is known locally as 'the sepulchre', a 'penthouse tomb'. It is an iron-barred cell behind which the remains of the Cabell family are buried, including Squire Richard Cabell, once Lord of the Manor of Buckfastleigh. Behind the bars is a tomb with a huge white slab on top of it. It appears as though a lot of effort was made to keep the dead within their tombs.

Squire Cabell

Squire Richard Cabell lived during the 1600s and has been described as a 'monstrously evil man', ill-treating the local people. The family were staunch Protestants and made life hell for any non-conformists.

Story has it that Cabell sold his soul to the Devil in exchange for immortality. Some even say he murdered his wife. He died on 5 July 1677 and was laid to rest in the sepulchre. It is believed that on the night of his interment, a ghostly pack of hounds appeared from the dark moor to howl at his tomb. Since then he has been seen leading the pack of hounds across the moor every year on the date he died. Wishing to lay his soul to rest and to 'keep him in', the villagers built a large building around the tomb and placed a huge slab on top of the grave. However, now and then a strange red glow can be seen emanating through the iron bars, and there have been reports of a whole host of demonic creatures gathered around the grave trying to get the promised soul for their master.

Under the church is a large network of caves, and just under the tomb of Squire Cabell is a strange natural formation where a stalactite and stalagmite have joined to form what is known as the 'Little Man'. It looks rather like a man dressed in seventeenth-century clothing.

The system of caves is ancient, and fossils dating back to over 100,000 years ago have been discovered – sabre-toothed tigers and woolly mammoths. Photographs and some fossils are displayed at the William Pengelly Cave Studies Centre in Russets Lane (only opened by appointment). Due to an important population of horseshoe bats living there, the caves have been designated a Site of Special Scientific Interest.

It appears that the church has always been doomed – whether because of Squire Cabell or not we shall never know, but throughout its history it seems to have attracted evil. During the nineteenth century, the graveyard was apparently a frequent target for body snatchers, as it is a quiet location next to a convenient lane.

On Tuesday, 8 May 1849, arsonists broke into the church and started a fire which destroyed the vestry, part of the roof of the north aisle and the parish chest, and badly damaged the communion table. It was recorded that in 1884 the church was restored. The work included renewing the spire, which had been truncated by a previous lightning strike.

During the Second World War, some of the stained-glass windows were shattered by the blast from German bombs which fell nearby and then, on 21 July 1992, sometime around midnight, the church was broken into and a fire was started under the altar. This time the church was gutted, as water had to be pumped uphill from the nearest hydrant. By that time, the fire was so intense that the heat blew apart the old Norman font.

Although it has never been proven, some people blamed Satanists and Devil worshippers for the fire. For hundreds of years it was thought that black magic rites had been carried out at the church, at the Squire's tomb in particular. You will notice that the building which houses the tomb has a solid wooden door at the back, placed there to prevent Satanists from gaining entry.

In 2002 there was a trial archaeological excavation on the site which revealed three Anglo-Saxon burials, along with a semi-circular apse, and the foundations of an earlier church within the walls of the medieval structure. It is thought that this might have been the location of the original Buckfast Abbey.

BUCKFAST ABBEY

The original monastery at Buckfast was founded during the reign of King Cnut in 1018. Compared to the other fifty or so monasteries in England at that time, it was rather small and unprosperous. It isn't known for sure where the site of this original Saxon monastery was built, although, as aforementioned, a recent excavation at the site of the Holy Trinity Church in Buckfastleigh uncovered what appears to be remains of an Anglo-Saxon church.

Buckfast Abbey is mentioned in the Domesday Book but, from then until 1136, not much is known of its history except that it might have been in decline. In 1136, King Stephen gave Buckfast to the Abbot of Savigny, who established the Savignac Rule here.

In 1147, Buckfast joined the Cistercian order; there was an immediate transformation. The Cistercian observance was a return to the rule of St Benedict in its original austere form. All luxuries were taken away, churches were stripped of ornaments, the rule of silence reaffirmed and a vegetarian diet enforced. The Cistercian white habits were made from natural undyed wool. Buckfast Abbey itself was rebuilt in stone.

The thirteenth century was a peak period in the abbey's history. The Cistercians owned large areas of land and became the country's main wool producers. In 1236, the abbots and monks of Buckfast were admitted to the guild of Totnes merchants, and by 1315 they were sending wool to Italy, as were most abbeys in the country.

Evidence of the monks' farming activity can still be seen. The Grange Barn, now a residential building, was used to store and thresh corn, and on Dartmoor the remains of a small homestead were found where a lay brother was kept in permanent residence with a shepherd to help him.

During the time of the Black Death (1348–50), many of the abbey's buildings fell into disrepair, including the almshouses, which appear to have burnt down. There would have been no need for almshouses during this time as housing was plentiful and, due to the shortage of labour, wages were high. The buildings remained neglected for thirty years until the economy recovered.

By the fifteenth century, Buckfast Abbey was a wealthy landowner and was running its own guest hall, almshouses and school, as well as maintaining the parishes and the manors.

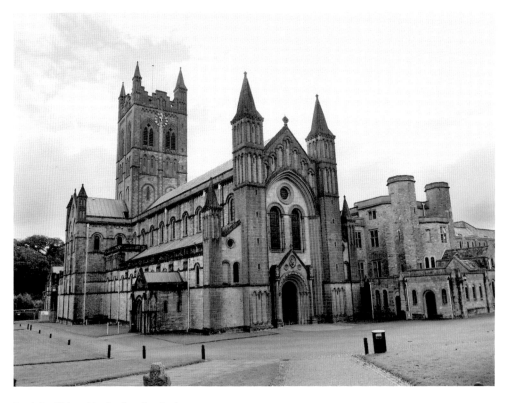

Buckfast Abbey. (Author's collection)

However, by the sixteenth century the monasteries in England were in decline. Henry VIII had noticed their wealth and declared them to be centres of 'manifest sin, vicious, carnal and abominable living'.

He appointed a new Vicar General and instructed him to reform the religious houses. On 25 February 1539, Buckfast Abbey was closed. Two of the King's Commissioners, William Petre and John Tregonwell, travelled the West Country and within four months they had closed forty monasteries, pensioning off the monks and taking possession of their wealth. In total they delivered 1.5 million tons of gold, gilt and silver to the Tower of London, which included the treasures of Buckfast Abbey.

The lands owned by the abbey were sold. William Petre bought the most prosperous manors, South Brent and Churstow. The abbey was vacated and its buildings stripped and left to decay. The five abbey bells were bought by the parishioners of Buckfastleigh.

Over the next 300 years, the abbey was bought and sold around four times until a group of monks, exiled from their monastery in France, took out a lease on the property with plans to restore it. In 1852, the monks arrived and began work. They uncovered most of the twelfth-century foundations and rebuilt the abbey in the style of the mid-twelfth century.

In 1906, Anscar Vonier was made abbot and announced that his first project would be the rebuilding of the Abbey Church. On 5 January 1907 he laid the first stone. The project took thirty-two years to complete and the last stone was laid on 24 July 1937. Abbot Vonier died just after the scaffolding was removed but he had fulfilled his wish of seeing the church rebuilt. A bronze plaque dedicated to his achievements can be seen in the south aisle.

Today the abbey is self-supporting, with a farm where vegetables are grown and bees, pigs and cattle are kept. A shop sells wine, honey beeswax, fudge and other items made by religious communities throughout the world, and there is a gift shop, book shop, and restaurant for visitors.

On the west side of the abbey are two gardens, with plants ranging from herbs used in cooking or medicine to poisonous plants, and behind the public area is an enclosed garden for the monks. A bridge leads over the river to the abbey farm.

Buckfast Tonic Wine

This wine was first produced in the 1890s by the Benedictine monks at Buckfast Abbey using a recipe brought over from France, as indeed is the wine base used today.

The wine was originally sold in small quantities by the abbey itself, as a medicine with the slogan 'Three small glasses a day, for good health and lively blood'. In 1927, the abbey lost its licence to sell wine and the abbot signed a deal with wine merchants to distribute the wine on the abbey's behalf. The recipe was changed and the modern bottle carries a notice stating that it does not have the tonic properties of the type claimed in the former slogan. In fact, there is much controversy over the drink as it is a very sweet, high alcohol content drink which appeals to young drinkers. It also contains caffeine.

Whitethroat (*Sylvia communis*)

This little warbler is found on the heaths, on the edge of woodland and on farmland. It used to be a very common summer bird, flying in from Central Africa every year until its numbers started to dwindle around the end of the sixties, probably as a result of droughts in its winter home.

The male builds the nest, or several nests, which is a cup of dead grasses and roots lined with hair.

HOLNE

Holne is a small village that you'll pass through on the road from Buckfastleigh to Dartmeet. It originally developed during the eleventh century and now has a population of around 250, a church and a pub.

The Church of St Mary the Virgin was built around 1300 and was enlarged in the early six-teenth century. It doesn't look particularly elegant from the outside but the inside has some attractive features, such as a carved and painted rood screen and a matching pulpit.

In the churchyard stands a hollow yew tree, thought to have been planted around 1300; close to it is the grave of Revd John Gill, who was the vicar here from 1858 to 1917. He was ninety years old when he died. Notice the ancient cross in this churchyard – well, the ancient shaft of the cross – it has new arms and a new pedestal.

The pub, the Church House Inn, was built in 1329 and was once called the Tavistock Inn. The church has owned the inn since the eighteenth century.

The Holne Ram Roast

Every year on May Day the locals carried out a traditional ritual which became known as the Holne Ram Roast. A wonderful description of the day was written in 1853 by the curate of Holne:

> At the village of Holne, situated on one of two spurs of Dartmoor, is a field of about two acres, the property of the parish and called the Ploy Field. In the centre stands a granite pillar six or seven feet high. On a May morning, before daybreak, the young men of the village assemble there and then proceed to the Moor, where they select a ram lamb, and after running it down, bring it in triumph to the Ploy field, fasten it to the pillar, cut its throat, and the roast it whole, skin, wool, etc. At midday a struggle takes place, at the risk of cut hands, for a slice, it being sup-posed to confer luck for the ensuing year on the fortunate devourer. As an act of gallantry, in high esteem among the females, the young men sometimes fight their way through the crowd to get a slice for their chosen amongst the young women, all of whom, in their best dresses, attend the 'Ram Feast', as it is called. Dancing, wrestling and other games, assisted by copious libations of cider during the afternoon, prolong the festivity till nightfall.

It isn't known exactly when this ritual originated but the fact that a sacrifice at a menhir took place on May Day is indicative of a pagan ritual. Some people believe that the Ram Roast is an extension of the old Celtic celebration of Beltane (*see* p.117), which took place around May Day, the ram being a sacrifice to the god Belus.

Today there is a village fête on the Ploy Field, but the sacrificing of a ram does not take place.

Holne Chase

This is an area of steep woodland in the loop of the river between the two medieval bridges, Holne Bridge and New Bridge. On top of Holne Chase is a well-preserved Iron Age hill fort called Holne Chase Castle.

Common Hazel (*Corylus avellana*)

Recognised by its 'lambstail' catkins and hazelnuts, you can see this tree growing in hedges around the lowlands of Dartmoor. It grows in most areas in the UK, except on high ground.

Hazel wood has been used by man for centuries as it is strong and flexible. It was used in the building of wattle-and-daub houses, where rods were interwo-ven to form hazel panels called wattles. These panels were placed between two wooden posts, forming the frame of the house, and the daub (a mixture of mud and straw) was applied.

Hazel bushes were coppiced (cut back to ground level) every seven years, so there was always a supply of the slim hazel rods.

Today, hazel panels are used as fences. Hazel rods and living hazel are used for hedges around Dartmoor, the rods being woven between living branches which are bent over. Hazel rods are also still used today in basket weaving.

DEAN PRIOR

A large area of the parish of Dean Prior lies within the Dartmoor National Park. The village of Dean was cut in half when the A38 was built, and consists of Lower Dean and Higher Dean. Including the nearby hamlet of Deancombe, the population is around 160 inhabitants.

Under the influence of Buckfast Abbey the area was prosperous with wool production, but tin mining also played a part in its history. A cave at Deancombe, by Deancombe Brook, was clearly a tinners' hut used as a place of concealment by the tin miners. In the same locality, a beehive hut and a tinners' mill can be found.

The Weaver of Deancombe

Years ago in the hamlet lived a highly skilled weaver called Knowles. Knowles was probably the best weaver around and became very rich through his trade. However, he wasn't happy and, in fact, was rather a nasty character, being greedy, selfish and malicious to his neighbours. He was disliked by everybody in the area.

When he died he was given a wonderful burial and sent off in style, despite not being popular. His son Fernley, a caring and generous man, made up his mind on the evening of the funeral that he would continue his father's trade but would make amends for all his horrible deeds. When he woke up the morning after the funeral, he came down to light the fire and make his breakfast –

Dean Prior. (Author's collection)

but was astonished and shocked to hear the distinct thumping of his father's loom coming from the weaving loft upstairs. Horrified, he ran up and peered through the half-open door. There was his father, sat at his loom, weaving just as he always had.

Knowing he needed help, Fernley ran at full speed to the church to fetch the parson. Gathering his Bible, a candle and a bell, the parson followed Fernley back to his home and together they stood and listened at the bottom of the stairs. The parson, an expert in such matters, called out: 'Knowles, come down here at once. This is no place for a lost soul. Come down and return to your grave.'

'I will, as soon as I have worked out my quill,' replied the dead weaver. (A quill being a shuttle full of wool.)

'Nay!' shouted back the parson, 'Come down now! Your life's work is done.'

Amazingly, the ghost left his loom and came down the stairs. The parson threw a handful of earth from the churchyard into the ghost's face, chanting a prayer and ringing his bell at the same time. Immediately the ghost transformed into a huge black dog.

'Follow me,' commanded the parson, and the three of them walked out of the house and entered the nearby Dean Wood. The parson led them to a pool formed by the Dean Brook and, picking up an acorn shell, he said to the dog, 'Take this shell and when you have emptied the pool of water your soul shall rest in peace.'

To this day, local people never go near the pool at midday or midnight. It is said that when the church bells strike twelve the black dog can be seen furiously baling out the water from the pool.

SOUTH BRENT

South Brent is found in the southern edge of the moors, just by the A38. It is a large village, which is now mainly residential, with a thriving community, shops, pubs and a few businesses. Its name originates from the nearby Brent Hill (Brent meaning steep).

The Saxon stonework in the lower part of the church tower provides evidence that the village developed during Saxon times. It was recorded in the Domesday Book as belonging to the Abbot of Buckfast, along with its surrounding parish. It had been endowed to the abbey by King Cnut, shortly after the monastery's foundation in 1018.

In 1247 the village was recorded as having a church and seven houses. Although it was small, it was the centre of one of the richest manors in the area. Under the influence of the abbey, the economy was based mainly on the wool trade and sheep farming and flourished during the thirteenth and fourteenth centuries. In 1350 it was large enough to become a town, and a Royal Charter was granted to the abbot to hold an annual three-day fair on the land between the village and Brent Hill which brought trade into the village.

However, South Brent's growth wasn't maintained as other towns outgrew it. Totnes and Ashburton flourished as trading centres as their populations were more prosperous.

With the Dissolution of the Monasteries, William Petre, one of the King's Commissioners, bought the parish of South Brent. It was then one of the richest manors owned by the abbey and clearly sustained a good economy as there were five mills built in the village, one of which ended up being the home of Dartmoor author William Crossing. Various small industries thrived, including the quarrying of granite and slate, and a number of annual fairs were held along with a weekly pannier market which brought trade to the village.

During the fifteenth century, the village became an important staging post when the road between Exeter and Plymouth was turnpiked (made into a toll road).

With the coming of the railway in 1848, the village became a goods junction and a main line junction for the Kingsbridge line. However, the station closed in the 1900s and its importance as an industrial centre dropped. It is now mainly residential.

St Petroc's Church, South Brent. (Author's collection)

St Petroc's Church

The Saxon stonework at the base of the church tower indicates that this church was built on the base of the original Saxon church tower. A Norman cruciform building was then built, retaining the original tower at its centre and, over the years, the design has been changed along with alterations to doors and windows. Of particular interest is the twelfth-century red sandstone Norman font and the stocks in the porch.

You will also see that there is a blocked-up door – a reminder of the tragic day in 1436 when the Revd John Hay was dragged out through the door in the middle of his service and murdered.

The Brentathon

This is a successful two-day event that takes place every year in November. It includes live music and poetry. More recently, a Rockathon has developed – a rock gig for local bands. This starts on the Friday before the Brentathon.

Yellowhammer (*Emberiza citrinella*)

Common in areas of grassland fields and hedgerows, this small bunting has a bright yellow head and breast, and a chestnut back with black streaks. His chestnut rump and white tail feathers differentiate him from the cirl bunting. Yellowhammers feed mainly on the ground, but like to perch on telegraph wires and bushes to sing.

The female builds the nest, which is a cup of grass, plant stems and moss, lined with grass and hair, built on the ground in a place where it is concealed by overhanging plants. She lays three to four eggs.

Brent Moor

Up on the high moor, behind South Brent, is Brent moor, covered with old Bronze Age settlements. Clusters of hut circles are dotted about and at Corringdon Ball you can see a stone row and a chambered tomb.

SHAUGH PRIOR

In AD 700, a few groups of Anglo-Saxons settled on the south-west edge of Dartmoor, in what is now known as the Shaugh Prior parish. They cleared the land to form fields, which were divided into strips and allocated to the individual families. Some of the fields are still in this shape today. The village of Shaugh Prior was one of these settlements, and grew up along with other small hamlets in the area – all of which are referred to in the Domesday Book. The name derives from the Old English word 'escaga' or 'sceaga', meaning copse. 'Prior' became part of the name because the manor in which it was located belonged to the Plympton Priory.

By the eleventh century, warreners were established on the moor in this area and today you can see plenty of evidence of their work at Trowlesworthy and Hentor. Between 1200 and 1348 the population grew rapidly and this is possibly when the hamlet of Wotter first evolved, as population pressure drove people to seek other areas to farm. Tin mining was an important industry, with the tin being extracted from the streams and rivers, and you can still see the hummocks along the bank of the River Plym, evidence of the waste tips left by these early miners.

As the population grew and farms expanded, the surrounding moorland was enclosed and divided into fields. The community prospered due to clay mining at Lee Moor and Wotter, and records show that by 1883 there were five clayworks and manufacturers in the Lee Moor area, producing goods such as bricks and sanitary ware. The clayworks thrived throughout the twentieth century and remain in operation today. A tramway was built to take the clay and goods to Plymouth and this can still be seen now.

By the middle of the nineteenth century, Shaugh Prior was virtually self sufficient and the parish directories listed blacksmiths, millers, shopkeepers, shoemakers, inn keepers and 400 people employed in the clayworks. Eventually however, as with many of these small villages and towns, the opening of the railway and bus routes meant people could travel to get their shopping elsewhere and slowly the shops and services disappeared. By 1930 it was no longer self sufficient.

The Church of St Edward

The first church was built during the eleventh century and, for some reason, was built away from the majority of the inhabitants. It has been suggested that it was built here as it is on the route many monks took to and from Buckfast Abbey; stone crosses mark the routes close to the church. The existing Church of St Edward, with its tall granite tower, dates back to the fifteenth century, with the Church House being one of the oldest houses in the village.

Shaugh Prior Woods

On the steep sides of the valley, where the River Meavy and the River Plym converge, there is beautiful ancient woodland, which has now been designated a Site of Special Scientific Interest. Within it you can see mainly oak trees but also ash, beech, birch and alder. Many forms of lichen and moss grow here and the rich plant life includes bilberry, bramble, wood sorrel, heath bedstraw and various grasses. You may also spot a buzzard, a tawny owl, a great spotted woodpecker or a grey wagtail.

Common Alder (*Alnus glutinosa*)

Growing along riverbanks, this tall tree thrives in wet ground and has been growing in Britain for thousands of years.

Once upon a time the alder was feared because when the wood is cut it turns a blood-orange colour, causing people to believe the tree was the embodiment of an evil spirit. The Erlkönig (the Alder King) of the old German legend was such a spirit.

Alder roots contain bacteria which utilises nitrogen from the air and 'fixes' it, making up for the lack of nitrogen in the wet soil. The wood of the alder is yellow when seasoned and was used for clog making. It is now used for broom handles and the bark, fruit and leaves can be made into dyes.

Dewerstone Hill Fort

Dewerstone Rocks is a stunning craggy tor with a large rock at the summit and a large craggy rock-face called the Devil's Rock to one side. The tor takes its name from Dewer, the dreaded huntsman who was really Satan in disguise. There are three pillars of rock which are very popular with climbers, the highest being around 150ft tall, and the Royal Marines used to train their men to rock climb here, but the rocks can be dangerous and a number of people have fallen to their deaths.

On top of the tor is a Bronze Age hut circle, and the remains of field systems can be seen, so it does seem that prehistoric man settled here. Some have suggested that the peak was also once an Iron Age hill fort.

The Legend of the Dewer

Years ago there was a huntsman named Dewer, also known as 'the horned man' or the Wild Huntsman. He had an extremely ferocious pack of hunting dogs known as the Whist Hounds. It is said that when a storm rages across the moors, the Wild Huntsman is riding out and it is best to stay in. He doesn't only hunt animals, as he hungers for human blood and will drive men over the Devil's Rock, the cliff-face of the Dewerstone Rock. His hounds are reportedly white and huge, and have eyes and ears the colour of flames. If you are unlucky enough to come across them, you will allegedly get ill and die within a year.

Dousland

Dousland is an old mining settlement a mile to the west of Burrator Dam. In the nineteenth century, as Plymouth boomed and expanded, it was clear a new water supply was required as Drake's Leat was no longer providing enough and suffered from evaporation in the summer and freezing in the winter. A dam was constructed on the west edge of Sheeps Tor in 1893, and in five years Burrator Reservoir opened.

The Burrator Inn is a relatively recent Dartmoor inn, of around 100 years old, located about a mile and a half below the cattle grid at Peek Hill.

Yennadon Cross

Set back from the roadside, where the road from Princetown to Yelverton crosses the road from Walkhampton church to Burrator Reservoir, you will find the Yennadon Cross. It is rather damaged, with one arm knocked off, and was clearly used as a gatepost – you can still see the gate hanger at the bottom. The cross was found in the roadside wall, on the right-hand side of the road from Dousland to Walkhampton. A Mr Masson Phillips arranged for it to be recovered and set up at its current site in 1974. There is a socket stone about 600 yards down the road, at the entrance to the lane leading to Burnham Farm, which used to hold the cross.

SHEEPSTOR

The first written evidence of the village of Sheepstor is when it was recorded in a 'pipe roll' in 1168 as Sitelestorra. The pipe roll was the financial records maintained by the Treasury from the twelfth century until 1833.

Sheepstor has had several names over its lifetime. In 1262 it was Skytelestor, in 1474 it was Shittestore, in 1547 it was Shistor and in 1620 Shetelstor. It is thought that the first version of its name derived form the Old English word 'scytte', meaning bar or bolt, maybe reflecting the nearby profile of Sheeps Tor.

Sheepstor Church

Sheepstor church is full of fascinating features. The church itself dates back to around 1450. It appears that it wasn't dedicated to anybody until 1940, when the well of St Leonard is documented. It was built from the moorland granite with the window mullions made from white elvan, which was quarried on Roborough Down. (Elvan is a name used in Cornwall and Devon for the native varieties of quartz-porphyry, a very fine building stone. Another name for it is greenstone. It is often used for parts of buildings such as doorways, so they can be finely carved. Most of the elvan quarries are now disused.)

The church has six bells and inscribed on one of them is: 'I call the quick to church and the dead to the grave.' It is the ropes from this church that were supposedly used to measure the depth of Crazywell Pool once upon a time.

There is an old cross on some paving stones on the way into the church, the Sheepstor Village Cross. The stem was found in a field at Burrator while the base was lying in a hedge. In 1910, the cross was restored by the Revd Hugh Breton to commemorate the Coronation of King George V. The origins of the cross are vague but it is thought that it was St Rumon's Cross.

The church is approached through a lychgate. Coffins would be rested on the lychstone whilst waiting to enter the church. Inside the building is a strange sculpture which is now enclosed in a glass case. There is some debate as to its origin. It is a skull with ears of corn coming out of its eyes and is perched on an hourglass.

On the south wall of the church you can see a carpet hanging up. It is a Pua Kumba, a ceremonial blanket. It was given to the church by Dr James Masing, assistant tourism officer, when he came to visit the graves of the Brooke family in March 1996. He presented it as a gift from the people of Sarawak. A Pua Kumba acts as a sacred space in ceremonies and rituals performed by the Iban Tribe. It is used in weddings and funerals as a space that mediates between the spirit world and the world of the living.

Other Church Stories

Back in the 1800s, Mr Smith, the visiting vicar of Sheepstor, was apparently spending a lot of money on wine for the Holy Communion each year (between £1 and £3). He only had a small congregation and Holy Communion only happened once a year, so this was a huge amount of wine per person. The reason was finally uncovered, however. Mr Smith was a generous man and it appeared that after his services he would sit outside the church on an old stone seat, with various members of the congregation, and have lengthy chats – whilst drinking the wine.

Another story goes that, one day, a visiting vicar wasn't allowed into the church, despite wanting to give a service. He was told that a goose was sitting on her eggs on the pulpit and that it would be a terrible shame to disturb her.

The Bullring

In the field behind St Leonard's Well lies a 5ft-long slab of granite, which has the original Sheepstor bullring still attached to it. Apparently, after church, a bear or a bull was tied to the ring and set upon by bull dogs. This was entertainment. If any of the dogs died they were buried under the stone pillar. The villagers would have a festive time amongst the tombstones in the churchyard, buying ale from the old ale house next door. Today, the village hall is on the spot of the old ale house.

Crazywell Pool

Crazywell Pool is located just off the path from Burrator Reservoir to Whiteworks. It is a large pool of around 100m long – thought to be the result of tin excavation. It is fed by a hidden spring and, due to subterranean drainage at its lower end, its level doesn't rise or fall very much.

As there are no natural lakes on Dartmoor, this pool has attracted a few stories. It was once thought to have been bottomless and, according to parishioners, the bell ropes from Sheepstor church were once tied together to test its depth. The end of the chain of ropes was weighted and dropped into the pool. It didn't reach the bottom and so the conclusion was that it didn't have one. In 1844, however, the Plymouth Dock Water Co. drained the pool to supplement the Devonport Leat and a bottom was discovered – only 4.9m down.

Legend has it that anyone visiting the pool at midnight on Midsummer's Eve can look into the water and see an image of the next person in the parish to die. The legend has been around for years but nobody has wanted to try out the theory – except, that is, for two young men who were once visiting the area. They were in the local pub one night and heard somebody telling the story. Scoffing and laughing, they said it was total nonsense and surely nobody believed things like that happened in real life. At that, the locals offered them a challenge. They dared the two young lads to journey up to the pool at midnight on Midsummer's Eve and prove it wasn't true. The two lads accepted, of course. The night was dry and clear and the two lads loaded their bags with sandwiches and beer, then set off on their motorcycle to the pool.

Nobody knows what they actually saw in the waters, because on their way home they sped off the track and were both killed.

Gorse or Furze

The yellow flowers of the gorse bush are nearly always in bloom and the warm smell of cocoa they emit is a sign it is high summer, their hairy black seed pods bursting happily to spread their seeds. The gorse bush is very hardy with thick spiky leaves – which can give you a painful prick should you brush against them – and makes a good nesting place for birds, such as the linnet and stonechat, as it gives a thick protective cover.

There are two types of gorse and they both grow on Dartmoor: European gorse (*Ulex europaeus*) and Western gorse (*Ulex gallii*), the latter having more rounded leaves and flowering late in the summer.

The yellow gorse flowers were used years ago as a dye and the gorse bush was commonly used to hang washing on, as its spikes kept the washing from blowing away.

Drizzlecombe

To the south-west of Burrator Reservoir is a valley called Drizzlecombe or Thrushelcombe, brimming with ancient prehistoric monuments; in fact, it is a Bronze Age ceremonial and ritual complex and well worth the walk up to see it. You can get there by parking in the car park past Sheepstor, walking up to Gutter Tor, taking the path to Ditsworthy Warren Farm and, from there, following the path up the Plym Valley. Here you will see the monuments.

There are three stone rows here, all with a menhir (standing stone) at the end and a cairn associated with it. One of the menhirs is well known for being the tallest menhir on Dartmoor. It is 14ft 2in above ground (4.2m) and is also rather an unusual shape in that it looks a bit like a bone from one direction. Hence its name, the Dartmoor Bone.

In 1889, the site was surveyed and all three of the menhirs were lying down, including the 'bone'. It was re-erected in 1893 in its original socket hole. It has been suggested that it is aligned with its associated stone row in such a way that when the Winter Solstice ceremonies took place, its shadow may have been the signal of the commencement of the ritual.

Close by is a large but damaged cairn known as the Giant's Basin. Many of its stones were removed by warreners to enclose their warrens lower down the river at Ditsworthy.

Higher up the slope and overlooking the monuments you can see an enclosure of hut circles similar to the one at Grimspound (*see* p.149).

Yellowmead Down

Nearby Yellowmead Down is a Bronze Age stone circle consisting of four concentric rings inside each other, the largest being 20m in diameter, the smallest 6m. They once encircled a cairn. Clearly somebody important was buried here. To the south-west are what look like stone rows that are crossed by a tin miners' leat.

There are also plenty of pillow mound remains to be seen. This was obviously the site of a large warren.

Ugborough Moor

Judging by the amount of prehistoric remains scattered in this area, Ugborough Moor was another significant area in the Bronze Age. Crossed by the Two Moors Way, the panoramic views are stunning and there is an abundance of stone rows and hut circles. The two oldest known Neolithic monuments on Dartmoor are up here, two long cairns. They are located at Corringdon Ball and East Butterdon Hill. You can clearly see the remains of the long mounds of earth and stones, and the vestiges of the stone chambers at one end.

There are an amazing number of stone rows on Ugborough Moor – five single rows, one double row and a completely unique complex of seven rows. The stone row on Butterdon Hill is the second longest on Dartmoor at 1¼ miles (2km), the longest being on Stall Moor.

On all of the hill summits on Ugborough Moor there are large stone burial mounds (cairns), with further round cairns clustered around the summits. These highly visible cairns were either important burial sites or territorial markers.

Stall Moor

On Stall Moor stands the longest stone row in the world, at just over 2 miles (3.3km) in length. At the southern end of the row stands a stone circle known as 'Kiss in the Ring'. The circle is 51.8ft (15.8m) in diameter and consists of twenty-two stones, which are all in their original positions. The tallest stone, at 4.9ft (1.5m), is unusual in that it doesn't stand opposite the end of the stone row like most of the other circles and rows.

The Legend of the Dancers and Pipers

Legend has it that, many years ago, a group of local young people from the area went up to Stall Moor to have a party. It was on a Sunday and it didn't occur to anybody that God might be unhappy about this until they were in the middle of dancing and playing their pipes. When the realisation dawned that God would be displeased, the pipers made a run for it. They were each struck down by lightning and turned to stone as they fled, in a row, away from the dancers, who were transformed into stones whilst dancing in their circle.

Stalldown Barrow

This barrow lies to the east of the stone row. Many years ago, a small house known as Hillson's House was built right here by a clockmaker.

Hentor Warren and Trowlesworthy Warren

During medieval times, rabbits were farmed for their meat and fur. The meat was a delicacy, consumed at first only by the upper classes. However, as the industry grew, rabbit meat became affordable for everybody, even the poorest families. The fur was used to line gloves and trim clothes.

Rabbit warrening was extensive on Dartmoor and played an important part in its economy, especially in the south-west of the moors. Trowlesworthy Warren was one of the first. The main evidence left of warrening on the moors is what are called pillow mounds or artificial buries or burrows. These were built at the centre of a working warren. The warren was built by enclosing a wide area of moorland, either by building a wall or by using a natural barrier. Buries were usually built lengthways down a slope for drainage and then surrounded by a drainage ditch. They were cigar-shaped mounds, constructed by digging a narrow trench with smaller trenches coming off it. They were covered with granite slabs. On top of those, earth was piled up and covered with turf. A few holes were dug into the turf as doorways for the rabbits.

The buries had to be maintained, keeping the ditches clear and re-roofing them occasionally. To protect them from predators such as stoats and weasels, vermin traps were built. These were usually a box made of granite, with a sliding door of slate at each end. Walls were built as funnels to make sure the vermin ran into the trap. There are the remains of a vermin trap at the warren at Legis Tor and also at Ditsworthy Warren. Another feature left behind by the industry is the warren house, where the warreners would live. At the Trowlesworthy and Ditsworthy warrens, the houses still stand.

Warrening prospered until the winter of 1891, when the 'great blizzard' wiped out many of the rabbits. However, commercial warrening continued for another sixty-four years. Then, in 1954, myxomatosis killed about 99 per cent of rabbits. The 1954 Rabbit Clearance legislation saw the end of the industry completely.

Tormentil (*Potentilla erecta*)

Growing on the heaths of the moors, this little yellow flowering plant had many practical uses in the Middle Ages. Powder made from its roots was said to help with toothache and gum infections. Its roots were also used as a red dye to colour clothing, and also as an alternative to oak bark for tanning hides.

CLEARBROOK

The earliest houses in Clearbrook were built around 1846, on a field referred to in the deeds as 'Clearbrook Field formerly Parsons Field'. The name Clearbrook is possibly a reference to the stream that forms the northern boundary of this field; 'Clear' perhaps referring to the fact that the water wasn't contaminated with China clay like the other streams nearby.

Unlike most of the Dartmoor villages, there seems to be no apparent reason why people settled here. It appears that a man called George Frean owned the lands along with a couple of miners, so perhaps mining was the incentive. However, Frean sold the land. According to the 1851 census, twelve of the seventeen males who lived here were miners, but there were also farmers. This farming and mining community also had an inn, a railway station, post office, bakery and a few shops.

Now Clearbrook is mainly a residential hamlet, with only the Skylark Inn still open for business.

Drake's Leat

Running close by is the Plymouth Leat, also known as Drake's Leat. This was completed in 1591 under direction of Sir Francis Drake, then the Mayor of Plymouth, in order to transport drinking water over 18 miles from the River Meavy to Plymouth. The leat was a simple ditch and bank, which measured approximately 6ft at its widest and was approximately 2ft deep. Its course was gently sloping so that the water would not flow too fast and erode the banks. It took around thirty-five men just over four months to complete it. Drake took part in the ceremonial turning of the first sod in December 1590 and, in April 1591, the first supply of water flowed to Plymouth, with Drake riding a white horse ahead of the water all the way.

This leat supplied Plymouth for more than 300 years, until it was replaced by the Burrator Reservoir.

MEAVY

Meavy is a pretty village and a parish. The village is located beside the River Meavy, which eventually runs into the River Plym. Meavy actually means 'small river'. It has a central village green, around which some of its few houses are gathered.

The Royal Oak pub is one of these buildings – possibly the oldest, as it was actually once the Church House, dating back to the fifteenth century. It takes its name from the oak tree on the green which is apparently 800 years old. It is a traditional atmospheric pub with old flagstone floors, original beams and an open fireplace. Some of the seats are pews from the church. During the summer, drinkers sit outside the front of the pub and soon overflow onto the green.

Pedunculate Oak or English Oak (*Quercus robur*)

The 'king' of British trees, this majestic oak is native to the UK and Europe and has been revered as far back as Celtic times. The Druids held the tree as sacred, and gathered mistletoe from its branches for their secret ritual.

Its Latin name *robur* means 'sturdy', as before the introduction of iron-cutting tools it was virtually impossible to fell an oak. However, once it was felled, the strong durable wood was used to build the frames of houses and ships. It was grown into curved shapes for these purposes.

The popularity of oak wood meant that in Elizabeth I's reign, laws had to be passed to protect it. Oak trees were planted in royal forests to be used to build the Royal Navy warships, and today some of these old trees still grow there.

The oak tree lives for centuries and the oldest oak in the UK is believed to be around 1,000 years old. It has now become a national emblem in England.

Oak Apple Day

The English Civil War (1642-1649) was fought between the Royalist forces, loyal to King Charles I, and the Parliamentarians, led by Oliver Cromwell. The Royalists were defeated at the Battle of Naseby in 1645, and Charles I was caught and executed on 30 January 1649. Cromwell declared Britain a republic, 'The Commonwealth', and went on to become its Lord Protector. When he died in 1658, Cromwell was succeeded briefly by his son Richard, before the monarchy was restored and Charles II became king on 29 May 1660.

The future Charles II escaped from the Roundhead army after the Battle of Worcester, in 1651, by hiding in an oak tree near Boscobel House. This is known as the Royal Oak. When the monarch was restored in 1660, the day was commemorated by making it a national holiday, Oak Apple Day. People used to show their support of the monarchy by wearing sprigs of oak leaves or an oak apple. Children would challenge each other to show their oak sprigs, and those not wearing one would be punished by a pinch on the bottom or being whipped with nettles. The holiday was abolished in 1859.

The Royal Oak is the third most popular name for a pub in England and was also the name of eight of the Royal Navy's warships. 'Heart of Oak' is the navy's official quick march. The oak tree was also depicted on the reverse of the pound coin in 1987, and the National Trust use a sprig of oak leaves and acorns as their emblem. Oak wood is still in demand for modern furniture, as its silvery grain is an attractive addition to any home.

On Dartmoor, the ancient woodlands are oak woodlands, rich in life. Because the oak's canopy is open, plenty of light reaches the forest floor and the soft leaves rot quickly when they fall, creating a rich leaf mould in which other trees and shrubs flourish. These in turn provide food and cover for animals and insects.

St Peter's Church

Just behind the pub you will find the Church of St Peter, which dates back to AD 1122. There is evidence of the original Norman structure within the north wall and also on the chancel arch. At some time during the fifteenth century it was extended and then a further two restorations were carried out in 1873/4 and 1884.

When the third Sir Francis Drake (a descendant of the famous explorer) bought the Manor House at Meavy, he acquired rights over the Lady Chapel and had a doorway constructed of granite, leading into what became known as the Drake Aisle. The stained-glass window was given in memory of the Drakes, and it is said that the Drake family members are buried in a vault under the floor, beneath the brass plaque on the south wall.

Meavy Oak Fair

Every third Saturday of June the village green is covered with brightly coloured craft stalls, a barbecue, children's entertainers, maypole dancing, a dog show and, last but not least, a place to buy cream teas. This is the Meavy Oak Fair.

Crosses

Under the oak tree on the green is a cross with an ancient pedestal and shaft, and a new head. On the road to Lynch Common is Marchant's Cross. This ancient cross is relatively tall, with short arms. It is in good condition and you can see an incised cross on each side. It is thought that the name of 'Marchant' is possibly a corruption of the word 'Merchant', implying that the cross may have been the gift of a trader or wool merchant who would have regularly used this route. It has also been suggested that it marks the burial of a suicide.

YELVERTON

Situated on the A386 from Tavistock to Plymouth, Yelverton is a late Victorian and Edwardian village. The name is thought to have derived from 'Ellas Ford Town', contracted to Elfordtown. Close to Yelverton is The Rock, a large mass of stone on the fringe of Roborough Down.

During the Second World War an airfield was built here, and today you can still see the runways and the earth and brick bunkers which protected the aeroplanes from attack.

WALKHAMPTON

A small village on the western edge of the moors, Walkhampton is also the name of the parish – one of the largest on Dartmoor, along with the Forest of Dartmoor and Widecombe. Walkhampton lies on the Black Brook, a tributary of the River Walkham.

The notable buildings in the village include the Walkhampton Inn, which dates back to the seventeenth century, and the church, a Grade I listed building standing on an ancient elevated site. Rather than facing east it faces north-east, the direction of the rising sun on the longest day. The present building dates back to the fifteenth century and has been altered over the years. For 400 years it had no dedication, until in 1985 it was dedicated to St Mary.

Next to the church is the old Church House, dating back to the sixteenth century, now two semi-detached cottages. Originally belonging to the parishioners, it was managed by the church wardens to brew and sell ale straight after church services. Other purposes included being the Council Chamber, the place from which bread was distributed to the poor, a collection centre for local tithes and an inn on the route from Buckfast Abbey to Tavistock Abbey. In 1894 it stopped trading, but in the early 1980s it was opened again. This is probably the oldest house in the village.

The stone cross at the Church House has been restored, with its shaft put back in its socket on the verge opposite. The socket stone was found built into a wall near the Church House and the shaft was found lying in the lane leading to the church. These were brought together and erected at its current site in 1984, by a lady who lived nearby. The four holes on one side of the cross indicate that it was once used as a gatepost.

Walkhampton Common

On the moorland above the village, Walkhampton Common contains a diverse and scattered selection of archaeological sites of all periods. It is a prehistoric ritual landscape of around 4,000 years old, with around eight stone rows, as well as cairns, kists, reaves and hut circles from the Bronze Age. The Great Western Reave, to the west, is over 6 miles long (10 km) and probably marked the upper limit of the enclosed land. The area is a Dartmoor National Park Premier Archaeological Landscape.

In the southern and central area you can see the remains of the round houses (hut circles) which are clustered together with some free-standing, but the majority are within or around walled enclosures. There is plenty of evidence here of tin working from medieval times and later, with the remains of tin streaming activity evident along the River Meavy and its tributaries, the Har Tor Brook and Newlycombe Lake. Remains of open-cast mining activity can also be found along with important medieval tin mills and their leats. The Devonport Leat, constructed in 1789 to provide water to the Devonport Docks, passes through this area.

Sharpitor

Sharpitor can be seen from the B3212 and there is a car park nearby making it accessible. Close by the car park are many cairns and cists, and two stone rows – one double and one single. The double row travels around 100m, with many of the stones being difficult to spot. It ends at a cairn of about 7m diameter. The single row runs close by and is also difficult to make out, but you can see a nearby ring of nine stones which form the outer ring of a cairn.

Black Tor

At Black Tor you will see an example of a logan stone, and on the top you will find a rock basin. There are fabulous views from here, and all around are ancient monuments left by Bronze Age man.

Black Tor Stone Row

Below Black Tor is a double row of stones of over 280m long. It leads up to a small group of three cairns at its south-west end. The row itself is partly overlain with a more modern stone wall, which follows the same course. Many of the stones from the row are possibly lying in this wall. The stones stand at heights of between 50 and 80cm and are quite a bit larger than those in the rows at Hart Tor 500m away.

Hart Tor Stone Rows

Running up Hart Tor are a couple of stone rows, a double and a single. They terminate at a pair of cairns, one a ring cairn.

Yelverton church. (Author's collection)

'Black Tor.' (Miles Wolstenholme)

WEST DARTMOOR

HORRABRIDGE

Just off the A386 between Tavistock and Yelverton is Horrabridge, a pretty riverside village of around 2,000 inhabitants. It was situated where the boundaries of four parishes meet – Buckland Monachorum, Whitchurch, Sampford Spiney and Walkhampton – until it formed its own parish. Its name means 'bridge on the boundary', as the village grew up around the packhorse bridge over the River Walkham. The existing bridge was built during the thirteenth century but there is evidence of an older bridge beneath the road.

The River Walkham is famous for its salmon fishing and is one of the fastest-rising rivers in Devon. It was central to the village and used for farming, to supply the tin and copper works, to power the mills and to power an early hydroelectric turbine.

There is little surviving evidence of Horrabridge's medieval roots except the bridge and some remnants of the Chapel of John the Baptist. It is thought that in the centre of the village there was a market place, as the tithe map from around 1840 indicates a small market place just to the north of the existing Methodist church. It appears the market had gone by 1888.

The main industry of Horrabridge, up until the twentieth century, was tin and copper mining. Although the industry has disappeared, there are many unmapped shafts still in the village and the surrounding area, and there is evidence of an early tin processing site at Little Horrabridge. Various mills, dating back to the fourteenth century, were established in the village; they were originally corn grists. In 1850, one of the mills was used for wool processing for the cloth trade.

It appears that Horrabridge was a busy industrial centre during the nineteenth and early twentieth centuries, with an increase in the number of houses built. The number of post-war houses built has impacted the surrounding countryside and affected the character of the old village. It is now mainly residential, with two pubs, the Leaping Salmon and the London Inn, a post office, bakery, florist, a DIY shop and a newsagent.

Churches

One of the village's most outstanding listed buildings is the Methodist church in Station Road. During the second half of the nineteenth century, Horrabridge was made into an ecclesiastical parish (1857) and a consecrated church was established in the former Bible Christian Chapel in Station Road (the site of the present Church Hall). This church was replaced in 1893 by the Grade II listed church building dedicated to St John the Baptist.

Sycamore (*Acer pseudoplatanus*)

Growing to heights of 115ft (35m), the sycamore is Europe's largest maple. It grows all over the UK although it isn't native. It is often found near dwellings, as it forms a wind-break and shelter.

Sycamore is a hard wood and is creamy-white. It is easy to work and doesn't warp, so is popular for furniture and for musical instruments. In the past it was used for household utensils, and kitchen and dairy work surfaces.

The Martyrs' Tree at Tolpuddle, in Dorset, is a famous sycamore under which six farm workers met in 1834 to form a society to fight starvation wages. They were sentenced to seven years' transportation to Australia but returned two years later after being pardoned.

Sampford Spiney church. (Author's collection)

SAMPFORD SPINEY

Sampford Spiney is a small hamlet on the west of Dartmoor. The land once belonged to Plympton Priory and the monks used to call here on their way to Tavistock Abbey. It has been suggested that the name derives from 'Spinetum', which means a thornbrake or thicket of thorns. However, a man named Gerard de Spineto was the Lord of Sampford in 1154 and lived at the Manor House. His family lived here for generations and it is probable that the name led to the parish being called Sampford Spiney rather than just Sampford. In 1281 it is recorded as Sampford Spine.

The Manor House is mentioned in the Domesday Book and is known to have been around since before then. The earliest record of the house was in 1028. In 1581, Sir Francis Drake bought the house for £500 as part payment of a wager. He probably never lived here himself, and when he died it passed into the hands of his second-in-command, Mr Bosenham, who, under pressure from the Drake family, finally sold it to Thomas, the brother of Sir Francis Drake. The house was restored a couple of times and has changed hands since then. It was once known as Hall Farm after its then owner, the Revd John Hall Parlby. It later fell into disrepair but the present owners have lovingly restored it, and it is now a bed and breakfast and a small holding.

Huckworthy Common Cross

The monks from Plympton would have called in to visit the Lord of the Manor and the church regularly, and the Huckworthy Common Cross was a way marker. It is a basic cross, still in fairly good condition; there is just some slight damage to the north-eastern face of the arms, which have both had pieces knocked off them, making the already short arms look even shorter from this side.

Sampford Spiney Village Cross

Situated on the village green is an ancient village cross dating back to the sixteenth century. It is in relatively good condition despite it having once stood in a nearby hedge. It was moved to its existing location by Revd John Hall Parlby.

St Mary's Church

Behind the cross stands the church of Sampford Spiney; a very simply designed and pretty church, built in the thirteenth century, nestled in the woods. It was enlarged during the sixteenth century and the arms of Plympton Priory are still on the tower.

Sampford Spiney Woods

Sampford Spiney Woods is a Site of Special Scientific Interest; it is an ancient woodland of exceptional importance in terms of its wildlife. It has a huge diversity of lichens, and plants such as the royal fern and bluebells. The area is also noted for birds such as the dipper, grey wagtail and the redstart, buzzard and wood warbler. It is alive with life and the other rare and notable inhabitants are various kinds of fritillary butterflies.

TAVISTOCK

On the south-western edge of the moors is Tavistock, located on the River Tavy from which it derives its name. There are plenty of Bronze Age and Iron Age remains in the area; it is believed that a settlement existed here long before the abbey was founded and the town's official history was recorded.

The Abbey of St Mary and St Rumon was supposedly founded by Ordgar, Earl of Devon in AD 961. But another story tells that Ordgar's son, Ordulph, used to go outdoors every night to pray. One night, Ordulph saw a brilliant column of light in the sky which put a great fear in him. When he went back to bed and fell asleep he had a vision of an angel in white who commanded him to search out the place where the pillar of light had stood – he would find it marked out in a square by four rods – and there build a chapel to the four Evangelists. Ordulph told his wife of the vision, but it had to be repeated a second and a third time before he took action. When he did as commanded, he founded not only a chapel but also a large monastery. So, this is how Tavistock Abbey came into being. In AD 981 its liberties were confirmed.

Ordulph was a man of enormous strength and stature and there are huge bones, said to be his, still shown in the parish church of Tavistock. One story tells of Ordulph breaking down a heavily barred gate and part of the adjacent wall with little effort. He is also said to have been able to stride across a 10ft-wide river.

The abbey was wealthy, and flourished until AD 997 when the Danes sailed up the River Tamar, stole the riches from the abbey, burnt it to the ground and made off with their plundered goods.

Shortly afterwards, the abbey was rebuilt and was soon flourishing again. There were many benefactors and, in 1105, King Henry I granted the abbot a Royal Charter. Royal Charters were used to create towns and cities, i.e. localities with legal rights. With it came the right to a weekly pannier market and a three-day-long fair once a year to mark the feast of St Rumon. This fair now takes the form of the annual Goose Fair in October, and the weekly pannier market still takes place today.

A Stannary Town

In 1185 Tavistock had achieved borough status and, in 1305, was one of the four stannary towns appointed by a charter of Edward I. Several of the abbots were learned men and, soon after the introduction of printing in England, a press was established in the abbey; the second press in the country. The town prospered in the hands of the abbots, with its various fairs, and became an important centre of trade and religion.

The End of the Abbey

In 1539, with the Dissolution of the Monasteries, John Peryn, the thirty-sixth and last abbot, surrendered his monastery on being allowed the sum of £100 per annum for life. The abbey lands were granted by Henry VIII to John, Lord Russell, whose descendant, the Duke of Bedford, is now owner of its site and ruins. The abbey was demolished.

All that remains now is the north-east angle of the cloister in the churchyard (said to be part of the north wall of the church and called 'Ordulph's Tomb'); the east and the west gatehouses, the western one called Betty Grimbal's Tower; a pinnacled porch; and the frater, now converted into a Unitarian chapel.

Running along the river further to the south is part of the precinct walls and a tower called the Still-tower. At the northern end of the precinct, behind a row of houses on the east side of Market Street, is a private building which was inside the precinct and is reputed to have been one of the monastic buildings.

Mining

The Russell family were central to the town's growth and prosperity after the Dissolution, and the main industry at that time was mining. There were mines of copper, tin and silver in the area. Cattle, corn brewing and iron founding were also important to the economy.

By the seventeenth century, tin mining had declined and the cloth trade began to prosper – until the 1800s when copper mining boomed. The Tavistock Canal was dug in 1817 to carry the copper to Morwellham Quay on the River Tamar, where it was loaded onto sailing ships. Under the influence of the Duke of Bedford, Tavistock flourished in the nineteenth century. The Devon Great Consols Copper Mine nearby became one of the biggest copper mines in the world, and a copper statue of the 7th Duke of Bedford was erected in the Guildhall Square. The duke built a reservoir to supply the town with water and constructed 100 miners' houses for the workers at the southern end of the town. In fact, he rebuilt much of the town, including the pannier market buildings and the town hall. The 'Bedford style' design of the buildings can be seen across Tavistock and much of the local area to the north and west, where the Bedfords had their estate and Endsleigh House and Gardens.

By 1890 the population had reached 9,000. By 1901, however, the population had halved and was recorded as 4,728, probably due to the increase in competition from copper mines around the world. In 1911, the Bedfords sold most of their lands in the area to pay death duties and today the Town Council owns most of the land; in fact, the parish council is one of the richest parish councils in England.

Tavistock's Railway Stations

The railway was built in 1859, connecting the town to the Great Western Railway and the London South Western Railway. A second station was built in the north of the town. The two stations were closed in the 1960s. Tavistock South was closed and dismantled, and no sign of it remains. However, Tavistock North's main building still remains and is a railway-themed bed and breakfast. The goods yard is now known as Kolworthy Park; the offices of West Devon Borough Council are located here.

St Eustachius' Parish Church

Much of the history of this church is tied up with the abbey. The first official record of its existence is from 1265, although none of the original structure is left now.

Saint Eustachius was a Roman General during the second century; he became a Christian and was consequently martyred with his family for refusing to renounce his belief and sacrifice to the Roman gods. There is only one other church in England dedicated to St Eustachius, but he is the patron saint of Madrid and there are dedications in Paris, Rome and Istanbul.

The church was completely rebuilt in 1318 by Abbot Robert Champeaux and had to be restored at the end of the fourteenth century after falling into disrepair. Further work was carried out during the fifteenth century and the Clothmakers Aisle was added in 1447, funded by a bequest from Constance Coffyn, widow of three wealthy wool merchants. The clock and chimes are interesting in that they have a different chime for each day of the week. They were given to the town and are now the property of the Town Council.

The Legend of the Abbots Way

Years ago, the three wealthiest abbeys around Dartmoor were those of Tavistock, Buckfast and Plymstock. All the monks from these abbeys were on friendly terms and would regularly pay each other visits – that was until one day there was a disagreement between the monks of Tavistock and the monks of Plymstock. When it appeared that the disagreement wasn't going to be easily resolved, Walter, the Abbot of Tavistock, decided he would travel to Plymstock to resolve the dispute once and for all.

As soon as he set off on his journey, a group of the younger monks from his abbey decided they deserved some fun, as life was pretty harsh with him as abbot. They decided to drink all the wine from the abbot's cellar and, when this had gone, they purchased some more from Buckfast Abbey.

Now, the most rebellious of this group was called Milbrosa and he was particularly enjoying his freedom. One day, when he was rather drunk and feeling like he could do anything, he took the silver communion vessels from the Abbey Church and sold them to the local gypsies – then spent the money on more wine.

Once he had sobered up he realised the severity of his actions and confessed to his friends. The gypsies had long gone, so one of the monks suggested they paid a visit to the rich old man who owned a blowing house nearby, thinking he might lend them enough money to buy back the silver. As they approached his house they saw him coming towards them, his packhorse laden with sacks. Envisioning the sacks being full of tin or copper, or even gold, the greedy monks decided to jump on him and rob him of his sacks. They ran to a spot from which they could ambush him.

When the old man reached the spot where the monks lay in wait, they rushed out, grabbed his sacks and killed him and his horse. Filled with selfish relief, the monks set off to recover the silver with not the slightest remorse for the old man and his horse.

The next day, a messenger from Buckfast Abbey arrived at Tavistock with a message from the abbot requesting some monks to join him immediately to witness a wonderful miracle. Of course, the group of greedy young monks jumped at the chance and put themselves forward to go.

It was beginning to get dark, so they mounted their horses at once and set off after the messenger into the drizzle and gloom. After a while, the messenger stopped and the moon came out from behind a cloud. They were stricken with fear as they saw that they were on the spot where they had murdered the old man. They looked at the messenger in horror as he threw back the hood of his cloak, revealing the face of the old man himself. In front of their eyes he turned into a skeleton with hollow, eyeless sockets fixed upon them. He beckoned to them to follow him and, hypnotised, the young monks walked forward and disappeared into a deep bog. They were never seen again.

When they didn't return and Walter discovered what they had been up to whilst he was away, he was sure they must have gone out and got lost on the moors. He ordered a number of granite crosses to be erected, marking the path between Tavistock and Buckfast Abbey, so that no one else would ever get lost. This track can still be followed today and is now known as the Abbots Way.

Greater Butterfly Orchid (*Platanthera chlorant*)

Found in meadows, roadside embankments and grassy areas, this orchid has greenish-white flowers which give off a vanilla scent. Only insects with long tongues, such as butterflies and moths, can reach the nectar from this plant as they have a long-lipped front petal. Whilst feeding, the head of the moth will touch one of the stamens and the pollen mass will attach itself to its head and be carried to the next flower where it pollinates.

Woodmouse (*Apodemus sylvaticus*)

This is Britain's most common mouse and lives mainly in deciduous woodlands, although it is found in fields, hedgerows, gardens and even indoors. It is a solitary animal and nests in a corner or hollow somewhere, building its nest from twigs, leaves and anything else it may find. The female has two to four litters a year.

MERRIVALE

Travelling along the road from Two Bridges towards Tavistock, you will drive through Merrivale, one of Dartmoor's most well known and preserved archaeological sites. The area contains almost the whole variety of ceremonial monuments to be found on the moors and, as a result, was taken into the care of the State in the 1970s.

The name Merrivale was first recorded in 1307 as 'Miryfield'; 'myrig' meaning pleasant and 'field' meaning open space. There is certainly a peaceful feeling when you stand and contemplate the area. Here you can see a prehistoric ritual complex about 4,000 years old, consisting of four stone rows, a standing stone, a stone circle, several cairns and cists and at least one ring cairn. The Great Western Reave, a prehistoric boundary about 6 miles (10km) long, crosses the landscape, indicating the upper limit of the enclosed lands. This reave is unusual in that it has a number of cairns along its length. The reave and the settlement are around 3,500 years old. The settlement has been cut in two by the modern road but in total there are around thirty-seven hut circles (roundhouses) which are well preserved, in some cases with the doorways discernable.

Nobody really knows why and what this complex once was, although there are of course many points of view. From the archaeological perspective it seems that the circles and rows were erected in Neolithic times and that in the Bronze Age they were still being used. Several settlements were built here during the Bronze Age and it appears that the territories were defined by the reaves.

There is a wonderful menhir (standing stone) here dating from the Bronze Age and, once again, the reason behind it is unclear – possibly a way marker, a territorial marker, a grave, a cemetery marker, a focus for ritual activity or a meeting place.

One theory is that the stone rows were built in alignment with the setting sun as a kind of calendar. Although much research has been undertaken on this theory, it has never been proven, and it does make you wonder why people would go to such an effort to construct a calendar when they lived in harmony with nature and the natural indicators of the changing seasons.

It is clear from Merrivale that spiritual and ritual practice was very important to the builders of these ancient monuments. Maybe that is why they are a mystery to us. It is also clear that a great deal of social organisation would have been needed to build these features, and that implies a certain level of thinking.

As well as prehistoric features, there is evidence of man's later activity. There are the remains of a warren and tin mining activities are evident, with the remnants of an old blowing house and tin workings still visible.

Ley Lines

Another suggestion is that the rows were built along 'ley lines'. The theory of ley lines was suggested by a man called Alfred Watkins in 1922, when he noticed that ancient sites such as burial mounds, churches, menhirs etc. were built on invisible straight lines which connected them all. There were many theories as to what these 'ley lines' were, and one was that the alignments were above underground watercourses or energy sources.

Hundreds of separate lines have since been uncovered around the world, connecting ceremonial sites and sites of cultural interest, and it is now obvious that there was nothing accidental about the way ancient people sited their monuments. In England, the name 'ley' derived from the fact that many of the site names ended with 'ley'.

In France and Greece, many ley lines have also been plotted and the distances and angles between them are geometrically perfect – in some cases aligned exactly with main constellations. This perfection shows us that the ancient communities who built the sites had a very different view of the world to us; their bodies and brains were clearly more attuned to the earth and planetary alignments.

Dowsers at Merrivale plotted the ley lines there, and they match remarkably well with the sites of the rows, stone circles and standing stones.

The Wheatear (*Oenanthe oenanthe*)

This little bird can be seen flitting low over the ground to perch on a rock or boulder, with its vivid white rump for all to see. Its distinctive call is a vigorous warble mixed with rattling and squeaky notes. It migrates to Africa for winter and arrives back around the second week in March, sooner than other birds.

Dartmoor suits the wheatear as it builds its nest in the drystone walls or under large rocks, out of loose grass, stems and leaves.

PETER TAVY

Bronze Age hut circles at Wedlake, and enclosures on the moor at White Tor, are the first signs of settlement in this area. Peter Tavy and Mary Tavy developed together and it wasn't until Saxon times that Peter Tavy and Mary Tavy became two separate settlements. They were mentioned in the Domesday Book as individual villages.

There were strong links to Tavistock, only 3 miles away, as the Manor of Peter Tavy was given to Tavistock Abbey, which then passed to the Russell family, who later became the Dukes of Bedford.

Peter Tavy developed originally as a meeting place for farmers and workers leaving the moors to sell their goods. The road to Tavistock developed after the foundation of the abbey. Many of the farms can be traced back to the thirteenth century and it seems that many more developed in the sixteenth century. Some were more like hamlets, and two in particular were known to have had around forty people living there and working the lands. The farms were encouraged to expand and would not only be farming cattle and sheep, but also growing corn and rye as well as prospecting for tin.

'Merrivale Stone Rows.'
(Miles Wolstenholme)

'Merrivale in Winter.'
(Miles Wolstenholme)

'The Beckamoor Cross.' (Miles Wolstenholme)

Peter Tavy flourished during the seventeenth century and the church was extended. Along with farming, various other small industries grew. There were turfers here who would cut peat, stack and dry it and transport it to the tin mines for the blowing houses and stone masons who cut granite for a living. When the mines failed in the mid-1800s, Peter Tavy wasn't as affected as many Dartmoor villages, although the population did fall during the recession, as many of the miners went to South Wales and America.

You can still see signs of much prospecting for copper and arsenic along the banks of the River Tavy, with some open shafts and mining equipment still there, but none of the prospecting was successful. Today, as is the case with many of the small Dartmoor villages, most of the services have disappeared and few of the original families remain there.

St Peter's Church

The church is located near the Peter Tavy Inn. There is no physical evidence of a church existing here prior to 1185, but it is certain that one did. People had been living in the area since the Bronze Age and it is likely that a wooden church would have been built here when the Saxons were occupying the area. A Norman church replaced the wooden one, as is evidenced by the Norman face mask over the south transept window.

In the early sixteenth century, the tower was rebuilt and there is a record that in 1553 it had three bells. In 1673 the church was neglected slightly and there is a record of the rector complaining that, 'the church is neither wind nor watertight and has many woeful defrayments'. However, by 1692 it had been enlarged and hopefully was made watertight. There are many interesting features here to see; the font, the medieval rood screen remnants and the Tudor wood carvings.

At some time in the nineteenth century, the north-west pinnacle of the tower was struck by lightning. The roof was torn open and the gallery at the back of the church was nearly all destroyed. Emergency repairs were made at the time but there wasn't enough money until 1820 to renew the gallery, replace the skylights and refloor the church. Further restoration was carried out in the 1870s.

The burial register shows that over 2,000 people have been buried in the churchyard since 1614.

The Peter Tavy Murders

A newspaper report from 15 November 1892 tells of a tragic and true event that took place in Peter Tavy, known as the Peter Tavy Murders.

At this time, a young girl named Emma Doidge lived in Peter Tavy. She was seventeen years old and had a lovely brother, William, and a younger sister, Elizabeth. They were a happy family and all of the children sang in the church choir.

Also living in the area was a young man called William Williams. He was twenty-one years old and for a year or so had been infatuated with Emma. She wasn't interested in him in the slightest and had to reject his advances on several occasions. Emma's brother was well aware of the situation and tried to keep the young man away from his sister. However, William Williams was obsessed.

Emma was in love with another William, William Rowe, who lived nearby, and they would spend many an evening walking and talking, and sitting in the churchyard listening to the birds and watching the bats.

William Williams became insanely jealous; he couldn't bear to see Emma with another man. His obsession turned rapidly to hatred and his jealously turned to thoughts of revenge. So much so that one day he travelled the 3 miles to Tavistock and bought himself a pistol and some bullets.

By the time he returned to Peter Tavy it was getting dark and he knew that Emma was in the church at choir practice. Her brother had come along to protect her from Williams and, when he saw Williams approaching the church, they had an argument and Williams left again.

William Rowe was the organ blower at the church and later on, when choir practice had finished, Emma, her sister and brother, William Rowe and the rector, left to walk home together. Suddenly the rector realised he had left his umbrella behind, so Rowe kindly ran back to the church to pick it up for him as the others continued on their way. Emma waited for Rowe and the two of them followed on behind.

Suddenly, William Williams sprang out from behind a bush and pointed his pistol straight at Rowe's head. He pulled the trigger and Rowe fell instantly to the ground, dead. Screaming hysterically, Emma threw herself down onto Rowe in despair. As she lay there, Williams shot her in the head. Everything went silent, except for a few birds, and Williams suddenly realised the horror of what he had done as he stared at the still bodies. Overcome with remorse, he put the pistol to his own head. He pulled the trigger but amazingly only managed to wound himself by grazing his skull. In desperation, he tried again and this time the bullet went through his eye – but he was still alive! In bloody torment, and wracked with pain and anguish, he ran towards the river where he threw himself into the fast waters.

He still didn't die. A local man saw him downstream, pulled him out and took care of him. He was taken to hospital and after clever surgery he recovered, except for his eye.

At the inquest of Emma Doidge, on 19 November 1892, the verdict was returned of Wilful Murder and, on 9 March 1893, Williams was sentenced to death.

Stephen's Grave

On the outskirts of the parish is a grave marked by a granite stone with an 'S' carved into it. This is allegedly the grave of a young man named George Stephens, who lived in Peter Tavy around 300 years ago. He was deeply in love with a beautiful local girl who wasn't in love with him and rejected his advances for another lad.

Broken-hearted, George Stephens couldn't see the point in living any more and took his own life. As with all suicides back then, he couldn't be buried on consecrated ground and was taken to be buried at a crossroads on the edge of the parish, so his soul wouldn't be able to find its way back to the village to haunt anybody.

Just at the moment that Stephen's body was being lowered into the grave, a freak gust of wind whipped a white linen sheet off a nearby washing line, taking it high into the air, and it was never seen again. Even today the locals don't go near the crossroads in the dark, as it is said that Stephen's tormented soul can be seen beside his grave.

Cox Tor

Above Godsworthy, on the north-east slopes of Cox Tor, you can see the remains of an ancient Bronze Age settlement. It consists of five enclosures and about twenty-five hut circles which aren't in very good condition. It appears that many of the stones were taken to build the nearby farmhouses and field walls.

White Tor

White Tor is similar to Dewerstone in that it has been recognised as being a Neolithic settlement site. There is evidence here of rectangular areas of ground clearance which are similar to those discovered in Cornwall. A nearby small-chambered tomb could also be associated with the settlement.

However, when the site was excavated in 1898/9 little was found other than a few flint stones, so there is still ambiguity over the age of this settlement. If it was a Neolithic settlement site then White Tor would be one of the earliest settlements on Dartmoor, and would be classified as a tor enclosure. A tor enclosure is described as a large hilltop or hill slope enclosure in South West England, located close to rock outcrops and surrounded by one or more circuits of stone-built walls.

'West from Great Staple Tor towards Cox Tor.' (Miles Wolstenholme)

During the excavations, there appeared to be the remains of double stone-built walls, within which appeared to be heaps of small stones piled up, forming cairns. There were also some hut circles which contained a large amount of flint flakes – maybe the home and workplace of a flint knapper (a man who sharpened flints). About a kilometre away, at Wedlake, a polished stone axe was found, and a polished greenstone axe was discovered at Baggator Brook about 2km away. Numerous flints, dating back to Mesolithic times, have been found here.

So, nobody knows for sure whether Neolithic man did settle on White Tor but it is well worth the walk up there, not only to ponder it for yourself but also to take in the stunning views.

Bell Heather (*Erica cinerea*)

Bell heather is very common on the dry heath of Dartmoor. However, it looks very similar to cross leaved heath which grows on the wetter hollows nearby. Bell heather likes poor, well-drained soils, often in the middle of damp areas, and has been cultivated for gardens as it grows well where other things don't.

MARY TAVY

DARTMOOR
Thoughts of fox and otter fill my head,
As I walk along the water's edge,
A robin stares at me from a branch
With an eye as black as a drop of wet tar.
Crimson and yellow capped toadstools
Promise a trip to remember, entice me
On a journey through rows of regimental pine
And twisted root of rhododendron
Into the gloomy interior that is wood,
Still, secretive, full of sap;
Blackberries clot with ruby blood
Collected on thorns
From passing veins and arteries,
And everywhere I sense the greenness
Waiting to grow over me,
Moss to clothe my trunk,
Ivy to bind my feet,
Brambles to hold me, still
As a spider's glistening web
Waiting for a fly.

Fenella Montgomery

Mary Tavy, like Peter Tavy, was named after its church and the river on which it grew up. The two villages grew up separately and Mary Tavy appears to have been a peaceful agricultural settlement at first, its underlying mineral deposits undiscovered until the 1700s.

Mary Tavy can itself be divided into two settlement areas, Mary Tavy and Blackdown. Mary Tavy, the older part of the village, contains scattered farmsteads and cottages along the valley of Cholwell Brook. As well as the farms, barns and cottages at Mary Tavy, there appears to have been a mill and two corn millers amongst the tradesmen listed in a directory of the 1850s.

Blackdown is situated on the ridge, and one interesting feature that can still be seen is the Kings Way. It was the Tavistock to Okehampton section of the route between London to Plymouth, and King Charles I's mail was carried along here. By 1720, a regular post service had been established along this route.

Gibbet Hill
On the road between Tavistock and Okehampton, on top of a hill, is the place where captured highway men used to be left hanging from the gibbet as a warning to other potential bandits. Consequently, this hill is known as Gibbet Hill.

The Church of St Mary
The Church of St Mary is a small and picturesque church situated in the old part of Mary Tavy, dating back to the fourteenth century, with its tower added during the fifteenth century. It was extensively restored in the nineteenth century but still retains many interesting features, including an old sundial above the porch, which has a wagon roof. The porch also contains the village stocks, which was made to seat four people. Inside the church you can see a wonderful rood screen and some modern, carved panels which represent the Station of the Cross. In the churchyard, William Crossing (author and expert on Dartmoor) and his wife are buried.

The Mary Tavy church and the Peter Tavy church are located 1 mile apart from each other. You can travel between them by walking along a pretty bridle path with a bridge over the River Tavy called the Mary Tavy Clam. Clam is the term for a simple bridge which is usually a tree trunk crossing a stream, or one slab of granite (*see* p.142).

Mining and Wheal Friendship
Mary Tavy's location on the edge of the granite mass means its geology is perfect for mining. Veins of copper, tin and silver were all discovered here, copper being the most important economically.

The earliest reference to mining is that of Wheal Friendship back in 1740. This was the most well known and prosperous copper mine on Dartmoor and was working from the late seventeenth century until 1925.

John Taylor, a mining engineer of great repute, played a major part in the success of Wheal Friendship and took over the management of the mine in 1798. He built the leats which took water from the River Tavy and brought it to Cholwell Brook. Here, the increased flow provided water for the numerous leats powering the many waterwheels. By the 1840s, the mine possessed seventeen waterwheels, the largest of which was 50ft in diameter, and there were eleven shafts. He also constructed the Wheal Jewell leat and was responsible for the building of the Tavistock Canal.

Taylor took great care of his workers, wanting to make their lives easier. He introduced a token system of payment which meant he could pay them with tokens if their wages were late in arriving. The 'Tavistock Tokens' could be used to pay for many goods and services locally and were then cashed in by the traders. Taylor also introduced the 'miners' dry', a building where the miners could leave themselves some dry clothes for when they came up from the mine. Here they could also clean themselves up. There is an example of a miners' dry at Bennetts Shaft but it is roofless and neglected.

During the mid-nineteenth century it appears that the population was booming in the area, although there was little housing. We can only assume that the poor workers were crammed into temporary shelters, shacks and hovels. A few houses remain today that were probably occupied by the bosses, but there is no evidence of the homes of the miners. The welfare of the miners wasn't a concern of the shareholders and many of them must have lived in hardship, danger and poverty.

At the end of the nineteenth century, competition grew from around the world and many miners left in search of their fortunes.

As well as being a well-known mining settlement, Mary Tavy is also known for its use of flowing water. In 1932, a hydroelectric power station was built using the leats left by the mining industry. It is still in operation today and has the power to provide electricity for 5,000 homes using the original seventy-year-old turbines, switchgears and gauges. Even in this time of finding renewable energy supplies, and despite the plant's success, it is still an exception and consequently a feature of industrial archaeology. It attracts regular visits from many educational and engineering societies.

Wheal Betsy

A well-known sight along the main road from Okehampton to Tavistock, Wheal Betsy is a ruined engine house of the ancient silver and lead mines. It was built in 1867 and restored in 1967 by the National Trust.

Arsenic and Mundic

At first, mundic was considered a waste product that had to be disposed of. Also known as iron pyrites or fool's gold, it was often found in copper and tin mines including Wheal Friendship. When the miners realised the value of the mundic, and copper started to become scarce, they turned their attention to retrieving what they could.

Women were employed on the surface to break up the mundic and they became known as Bal Maidens. There is still a Bal Lane in Mary Tavy today. The crushed ore was heated in a furnace and the impurity they were after, arsenic, was allowed to condense on the sides of the flues that carried the smoke away from the fire.

Arsenic is a notoriously poisonous material found in many minerals but mainly associated with metals. It has been used since ancient times, and during the Bronze Age it was used to make the bronze harder. Later, murders commonly involved the use of arsenic, as it was hard to detect. It was used a lot by the ruling classes and became known as the Poison of Kings.

During the Victorian period, women mixed arsenic with vinegar and chalk and ate it to make their faces paler – a sign that they didn't work in the fields. They also rubbed it into their faces and arms to improve their complexions.

In 1858, it was accidentally used in the production of some peppermint humbugs which were sold from a market stall and caused twenty deaths. This was known as the Bradford Sweet Poisoning and contributed to the introduction of the Pharmacy Act in 1868, which regulated against adulteration of foodstuffs.

It was widely used as a pesticide, in herbicides and insecticides, but these are in decline and the largest application of arsenic today is in alloying copper and lead.

The Zoar Bible Christian/Methodist Chapel

This small chapel was built in 1904 and cost £400. It is one of the last Bible Christian chapels to be built. In 1930, the ground on which it was built was consecrated and since then many people have been buried here. There is only a small congregation but an afternoon Sunday service still runs. The Bible Christian Church was a Methodist church founded in 1815 by a Wesleyan preacher called William O'Bryan. It was mainly based in Devon and Cornwall but spread to the rest of the UK with some missionaries even going as far as Canada.

The Reading Rooms

The reading rooms were constructed by Mr C. Doidge, with the intention of providing a place of relaxation, education and recreation for the local residents, and contained a comprehensive library supplied with a daily delivery of newspapers. It is now a recreation centre and the rooms are regularly used for snooker, billiards, darts and table tennis.

Peter Tavy Coombe

This is a local and popular beauty spot near to where the villagers have dammed the Colley Brook to make a swimming pool.

The Ring Ouzel

Found around North Dartmoor, the ring ouzel can be seen perched on far-off rocks and will give a loud rattling sound if disturbed. Part of the thrush family of birds, they have a white collar which is less distinct on the female. The male has a sooty black plumage and pale wing patches whilst the female is more of a brown-grey.

The ring ouzel is a shy bird and keeps itself to itself; at nesting times it can actually get quite aggressive if its nest is under threat. It will attack a crow or a buzzard, and even a blundering human can get struck on the head by the indignant bird.

Both the male and the female build the nest, which is similar to a blackbird's nest, and both the male and female will sit on the eggs until they hatch.

Reed Bunting (*Emberiza schoeniclus*)

Once upon a time these birds were only found on wetlands, but today they inhabit drier areas such as farms. This little bird is sparrow-sized but slimmer and with a long tail. The male has a black head and white moustache, whilst the female and wintering male have a streaked head.

They feed on insects and seeds and they still prefer the wetlands in which to breed, building their nests in a tussock or among dense vegetation close to the ground. The nest is a cup of grass and moss, lined with fine grasses, reeds and flowers, and usually the female lays four to five brownish-olive eggs.

NORTH BRENTOR

North Brentor is a village between Okehampton and Tavistock. The parish is called Brentor and the locals call the village itself Brentor, so this can sometimes be confusing. In total there are around 200 houses in the whole parish, seventy of which are in the village itself.

It is unclear when the village first developed, but there is evidence of prehistoric activities in the area and medieval references have been found. It was originally part of the Lamerton parish, and the Church of St Michael de Rupe, less than a mile away, would have been the first church used.

The economy was mainly based on agriculture, until the nineteenth century when it was influenced by the mining activities in the area. The growth in population and prosperity during that period led to the building of more houses, the school and Christ Church. A variety of tradesmen were recorded at that time; three farmers, three carpenters, one shoe maker and two shopkeepers. The railway was opened in 1865 and a proper station built in 1890.

Brentor Church

Just outside the village is the tor from which North Brentor derives its name, Brent Tor. It stands at 325m high and, unlike the other Dartmoor tors, it is made from volcanic rock which formed when the basaltic lava flowed out, around 350 million years ago, into the shallow sea which covered the area at that time.

The tiny church on its summit was built between 1152 and 1162 by Robert Giffard, Lord of Lamerton and Whitchurch. It was built using volcanic rock from the tor, known as 'spilite'. Lord Giffard eventually gave the church to Tavistock Abbey, along with some surrounding land, and in 1155 the church was dedicated to St Michael. It seems that many churches on high ground were dedicated to St Michael.

During restoration in the fifteenth century, forty skeletons were found beneath the floor; thirty-nine were lying north to south whilst one was east to west. West–east is the common

'Brentor Church.' (Mike Bartholomew)

alignment for Christian burials, so the dead person may rise on the day of judgement to face God to the east. It is generally assumed that an east–west and north–south alignment is a pagan burial. It appears that this may have been a burial site before the existing church was erected.

The tower was added or rebuilt during the restoration and you can see the inside drainage holes, which drain away any water seeping through the granite walls. There were only two bells in the tower during the fourteenth and fifteenth centuries, and a third was added in the seventeenth century. In 1909, all three were recast and two more added.

In 1958 and 1963, more restoration work was carried out on the bells. They were rung on many important occasions such as royal birthdays, accessions and coronations. They could also be heard on Oak Apple Day, Gunpowder Plot Day, and whenever the bishop passed by.

In the churchyard you can see the oldest sundial in Devon, dating back to 1694. On the southern side you will find the grave of Ingaret Stella Van der Post, who is apparently a direct descendant of Robert Giffard, the man who built the church.

The St Michael's ley line starts here and then heads north-west to Lydford, where it is intersected at Lydford Castle by a 'black line'. The line then flows to Brat Tor and Yes Tor and then to Belstone Tor, through the Nine Maidens stone circle, and then travels eastwards to an old granite cross near Ringhill Copse. This ley line is one of the largest in England and is aligned along the path of the sun on 8 May (the spring festival of St Michael). It runs through Glastonbury and Avebury.

The church has become a place of pilgrimage, with people coming here to find peace and stillness in times of stress. Services are held on a Sunday but if the weather is wet then they are held in the village church, as the climb is far too dangerous.

The church can be seen from Plymouth and from all over Dartmoor, and one letterboxer created a stamp called 'In sight of Brentor'. They are found all over Dartmoor.

The Legend Associated with Brentor Church

Years ago, a wealthy merchant was bringing goods up the Channel in his ship when the Devil decided to create a ferocious storm. There was no battling this storm; the winds roared, the thunder clapped and the lightning flashed. There was little the captain could do to control the ship as it was driven closer and closer to the jagged rocks.

The merchant, Hugh, knelt down to pray. He prayed to St Michael, promising that if his ship was saved he would build a church on the first high point of land that he saw. Amazingly, the storm subsided and the captain was able to sail to land safely.

The first high point of land the merchant spotted was Brent Tor and, because he was a man of his word, he commenced the building of a church as soon as he could, right on its summit. However, the church took a lot longer than he expected, not because of its location or lack of materials, but because the Devil had discovered what was happening and had become angry again. Each night he hurled all the boulders and building materials to the bottom of the tor; but every morning Hugh carried them back up to the top, determined to fulfil his promise.

After a while, the Archangel Michael came to Hugh's aid. He threw a huge boulder at the Devil one night, hitting him between the horns and causing him to leave Hugh alone at last. The church was eventually finished and, although it was much smaller than envisaged due to all the trouble from the Devil, it was complete and was dedicated to St Michael.

LYDFORD

The development of Lydford was unusual in that it was one of thirty towns, known as 'burhs', set up by one of the Anglo-Saxon Kings of Wessex, Alfred the Great. The kingdom included Hampshire, Dorset, Wiltshire, Somerset and Devon. Lydford was established in AD 890 as a defence centre against the Vikings and the Cornish. Its original name was Hlidan and then Hlidanford.

The site was chosen due to its position on the steep and close downward slopes to the east and west. Only the north side was vulnerable, and this is where the defence bank of stone and earth was built and can still be seen today. When the burgh was under attack, usually from the Cornish tribes, the peasants would congregate inside the defence boundary and each pole length (5m) of rampart wall was manned by four people. You can still see evidence of the Anglo-Saxon defensive earthwork wall, and the roadways are those from Anglo-Saxon times. The north–south main street of the Saxon town still exists through the village, along with many of the original side lanes.

The Lydford Silver Pennies

Between AD 600 and 1066 silver was the main currency, and Lydford became an important coin minting town, producing the well-known silver pennies of Lydford. There were rich silver mines in the area and coins were minted by expert metal workers called 'moneyers'. The coins were used throughout the Kingdom of Wessex, and each silver penny represented ones day's work for a Saxon peasant.

Every six years the coins would be recalled by the Crown Authority and coins of identical weight and size were minted and distributed with a different design. There are twenty-one different designs of silver penny in the British Museum.

Attacked by Vikings

In AD 997, the Vikings sailed into Plymouth and attacked Lydford (probably for its silver coins) before they went on to destroy the abbey in Tavistock. There is a plaque on the roadside at the southern entrance into the town commemorating this attack. Next to the castle in the field is a runic stone carved from local granite which was erected in 1997 to commemorate the 1,000th anniversary of the Viking attack.

It is interesting to note that, apparently, no Lydford pennies have ever been found in Devon. Sixty-eight Lydford pennies were found in Sweden, amongst a collection of 523 Anglo-Saxon pennies, but they were dated from between 1009 and 1016, so they were not from the attack in 997.

Lydford Castle

After the Norman Conquest in 1066, the first castle was built in Lydford. There were in fact two built; the first was high above Lydford Gorge, and now only the earth-covered foundations remain, along with a still-visible defence ditch. From here there are stunning views across Dartmoor and it is well worth a visit.

The newer Lydford Castle was built in AD 1195, probably as a prison. Its walls were 3m thick and two storeys high. During the thirteenth century the castle was rebuilt, and the upper storey was removed and replaced by two storeys with thinner walls of 2m. The base was covered with earth and stone to form a kind of dungeon and can still be seen today, looking like a grassy mound. A deep ditch was dug around this base for further protection. The whereabouts of the original entrance gateway isn't known but the present entrance is through a Norman-style archway. A bridge over the ditch would have led in from the courtyard of the castle (the bailey) on the west.

During the Middle Ages, the castle was used as a prison and a court of law. It was the administration offices for the Royal Forest of Dartmoor and also the Stannary Court, which had jurisdiction over tin mining in Devon and the behaviour of the miners. The laws were very strict and harsh, becoming known as the Lydford Law, whereby a person was hanged first then tried later.

During the English Civil War, the bottom of the castle was used as a prison where all the military prisoners were sent before being executed for High Treason. Throughout this time, the head of the court was Judge Jeffreys, known for being the 'hanging judge'.

Later, when Princetown Prison was built, the courts were moved there and Lydford Castle was abandoned. It fell into a state of disrepair. It is now owned and managed by English Heritage and can be visited free of charge at any time.

It appears that Lydford Castle was a gruesome place and is reportedly where the St Michael's ley line is crossed by a 'black line'. Dowsers claim that there is a very negative and evil energy here.

St Petroc's Church

Lydford church stands between the two castle sites. It is dedicated to the monk, St Petroc, who came to Cornwall from Ireland and travelled through the West Country in the sixth century. The younger son of King Glywys in Wales, Petroc was offered the crown of part of the kingdom when his father died, but he instead went to Ireland to study for a religious life.

The original building on this site may have been a simple wooden shelter where he rested when visiting. The first record of a stone church was in 1237, probably built by the Normans. Restoration and improvements were made during the fifteenth century. Inside the church are some interesting features; the ends of the pews are detailed wood carvings of numerous different animals. Outside the church is a well-known tombstone, that of George Routleigh a watch maker. His epitaph is now hanging up inside the church.

Lydford Gorge

Now owned by the National Trust, Lydford Gorge is a beautiful oak-wooded river gorge. In fact, it is the deepest river gorge in the South West. The River Burn plunges and tumbles through the gorge and an abundance of wildlife grows on the steep banks. It is 2km long and is a Site of Special Scientific Interest due to its geology and rock formations. The gorge was formed by the process of river capture (when a river or stream is diverted from its own river-bed and flows

'Lydford Church.'
(Miles Wolstenholme)

instead down the bed of a neighbouring stream). At Lydford Gorge, the start of the river eroded backwards until it intersected with the River Lyd, diverting its course into the second channel.

The Lychway or 'Way of the Dead'

The word 'lych' survived from the Old English (Saxon) word for corpse, and is used in modern English as an adjective in certain names or phrases. The lychway is the path along which a corpse was carried for burial. Other terms include 'lych wake' – a night watch over a corpse, and 'lych owl' – another word for a screech owl, its cry being an omen of death.

The lychway on Dartmoor is a well-known track that runs from the east of the moors to Lydford. Years ago, most of Dartmoor came under the parish of Lydford and all the burials took place in the churchyard here. This track was used by people carrying the dead to be buried and also for weddings, baptisms and services. Even when people no longer needed to travel to Lydford for burials, the path was still in use as the courts were held at Lydford Castle.

You can still walk along the track, but some parts of it are no longer visible.

Vigurs Eyebright (*Euphrasia vigursii*)

Classified as being of 'global conservation concern', this rare eyebright lives on Dartmoor where the grass is kept short by the grazing of the animals and by the burning of gorse and heather. Its main population is found on Lydford High Down, and suitable habitat management is taking place to ensure the survival of this plant.

Bray Tor and Widgery's Cross

Taking the A386 towards Okehampton, you can see Bray Tor off to the right, with Widgery's Cross perched on its summit. Bray Tor is 452m high and the cross is one of the tallest on Dartmoor at 12ft.

'Widgery's Cross.'
(Miles Wolstenholme)

The cross was erected by William Widgery in 1887 to commemorate the Golden Jubilee of Queen Victoria. It is different to other Dartmoor crosses in that is it made of several granite blocks rather than carved from one slab.

William Widgery was a well-known artist who developed his own unique style of painting. He loved Dartmoor and painted many landscapes, especially from the western side of the moors. His work became so popular that it was said each piece was sold before it left the easel. He built himself a house and studio on the edge of the moors where he lived for ten years. This is now the Lydford House Hotel. He died in 1893 and his son Frederick went on to become an equally well-known Dartmoor artist.

SOURTON

Sourton is a small village of around 400 inhabitants. It is known for two things – its interesting and bizarre pub, the Highwayman Inn, and its interesting stone cross.

The Highwayman Inn

The Highwayman Inn was built in 1282. In the seventeenth century it was called the Golden Fleece and was then renamed the New Inn by Plymouth Breweries. In 1959, Rita and Buster Jones bought the inn and called it the Highwayman Inn due to Rita's romantic notions of highwaymen dashing around in the mists of the moors. Rita and Buster set to work transforming the building, including using the old Launceston to Tavistock coach as the entrance porch. Work continued during the 1970s, '80s and '90s, creating what we see today – an amazingly characterful pub.

Sourton Down Cross

Sourton Down Cross also has an unusual past – especially for a stone cross. It is believed to have originally been inscribed between the sixth and eighth centuries, and was probably a memorial stone or grave marker, not a cross. Its first site at this time isn't known. Seemingly, sometime between the ninth and eleventh centuries the stone was moved and cut into the cross that it is today – with stumpy arms. It remained like this for 600 years until a 'directional marker' was needed and the cross seemed to be the handiest thing to use. That was when the 'H' for Hatherleigh and the 'L' for Launceston were inscribed on either side. Before the new bypass was built, the cross was situated on the old road between Okehampton and Tavistock. When the bypass was built in 1993 the cross was removed and re-erected where it is today.

The Ice Factory

In 1874, Mr James Henderson came upon the idea of starting an ice factory on Sourton Hill. He was convinced it would work and approached the Duchy of Cornwall to lease him part of the hill, so he could collect naturally occurring ice during winter. He envisioned a huge demand for ice as this was before electricity. After a few years of delay, he was finally given permission to 'form ponds and collect and store ice' on Sourton Hill for a term of twenty-one years. The annual rent was £10.

In 1875 the factory started production. However, after a few technical problems and then a couple of mild winters, the initial years weren't successful and, even though he did a few successful years, in 1886 Mr Henderson surrendered his lease. Eventually the ponds were refilled, fences taken down and machinery sold off. All that remains is another feature on Dartmoor.

Black a Tor Copse

A mile from Meldon Reservoir, up the West Okement River, you will find Black a Tor Copse, a small but very ancient oak woodland which has been designated as a National Nature Reserve. Its trees are covered in rich mosses and lichens and several species of nationally rare lichens grow here. Around forty-four species of mosses and liverwort have been recorded here and 133 different species of lichen.

Redstart (*Phoenicurus phoenicurus*)

Commonly found in oak woodlands and hedgerows, these birds have distinctive bright orange-red tails, slate-grey backs and black faces and wings. They bob up and down like robins but do not spend time on the ground.

In April the female builds the nest, which is a cup of dead grass, moss and bark, lined with hair and feathers. In the autumn they fly to Africa.

The Grimstone and Sortridge Leat

One of the most historic leats on Dartmoor, it is thought that this leat was originally dug to supply water to Grimstone Manor and Sortridge Manor. It is 11.3km long and takes water from the River Walkham, returning it to the same river lower down.

Today the leat is still important and supplies twenty-seven families, and a few farms, with water. However, in recent years the leat was losing water and sometimes drying up completely. It was leaking out of a section near Merrivale Quarry.

The Dartmoor National Park Authority and the Dartmoor Trust, who have formed a partnership to restore some of the Dartmoor leats to their original working condition, carried out repair work to the Grimstone and Sortridge Leat in June 2010. The leaking section of the leat was lined.

Yes Tor

At 619m, Yes Tor is the second highest tor on Dartmoor and is scattered with Bronze Age cairns. Its name was recorded in the 1200s as 'Emestorre' or 'Yemestorre', which derives from the Saxon word 'earn', meaning eagle.

'Black a Tor Copse.' (Miles Wolstenholme)

'West Mill Tor and Yes Tor from Longstone Hill.' (Miles Wolstenholme)

The remains of two cairns are situated on its summit (both of them now disturbed), suggesting that two important members of the prehistoric community were buried here. This area is used extensively by the military and there is a flagpole on top indicating when manoeuvres are in progress. The military started using this area in 1876 and have since widened and improved the existing moorland tracks and created new ones. There are a few military features to be seen around the tor, including three observation posts and an army hut, and at one time there was a telephone tapping point here to enable safety communications during training.

Frederick Widgery loved this tor and it features in many of his paintings.

High Willhays

A couple of feet higher than Yes Tor, and the highest point on Dartmoor, High Willhays stands at 621m. It is also the highest peak in England.

NORTH DARTMOOR

OKEHAMPTON

Okehampton is a busy town and is the gateway to the north moor. Narrow lanes converge onto a wide main street with plenty of shops and facilities for local residents and visitors.

Okehampton originally developed as a settlement during the Bronze Age. The name 'Ocmundtune', meaning 'settlement by the Ockment', was given to it during Saxon times. When it was invaded by the Normans, Okehampton became an important centre because Baldwin de Brion, the first Norman sheriff, built Okehampton Castle as an administration centre for his vast estates. Okehampton Castle is now owned by the English Heritage and is open to look around.

During the Middle Ages Okehampton thrived on the wool trade, as did most of the Dartmoor towns. Now it is a busy visitor centre.

The Museum of Dartmoor Life

The museum is an interesting place to visit to find out more about the way people lived and worked on Dartmoor. It was opened in 1982 when a group of local volunteers decided they needed somewhere to keep the growing collection of local objects they were accumulating. It is an independent museum and so charges for admission.

Legend of Cranmere Pool

Long ago there lived a wealthy merchant in the town of Okehampton. His name was Benjamin Gayer and he was a great and prosperous businessman who owned several ships which sailed around the world carrying his cargo. At this time piracy was rife and many ruthless pirates sailed the sea stealing goods, and also stealing sailors who they held for ransom. The people of Okehampton realised they needed to raise some money as a fund, just in case they needed to pay a ransom for one of their sailors, and Benjamin Gayer was put in charge of raising the money and managing it. With the generous help of his wealthy acquaintances he soon accumulated a fine ransom fund.

One day, one of Benjamin's own ships was attacked by pirates and all his cargo was taken – completely gone. What a shock for poor Benjamin Gayer – this cargo was all the wealth he had. Unless he could raise some money to buy more, he would be ruined. But nobody would lend him the money, saying it was too much of a risk.

In desperation, Benjamin Gayer decided he would borrow the money from the ransom fund. He meant to pay it back as soon as he made back his money. So, he bought some more cargo and set it to sail. However, as fate would have it, it was once again taken by pirates. Poor Benjamin Gayer was beside himself. Not only did he have no money but now there was no ransom fund.

'Okehampton Castle.' (Miles Wolstenholme)

What if a poor local sailor was kidnapped? He was distraught, wracked with guilt and remorse over what he had done. In fact, he was so remorseful that it made him ill and he soon died.

Even in death Benjamin Gayer couldn't find peace. His soul wouldn't rest and he roamed Okehampton every night wailing and moaning – so much so that the townsfolk started to get irritable, as their sleep was disturbed. Finally they decided to do something about it and they asked the archdeacon for help.

The archdeacon gathered together all the local clergymen and together they tried to send poor old Benjamin Gayer back to his grave. But his wailing, moaning and misery continued. Then the archdeacon remembered a very clever priest who lived on the moors and he summoned him to help. The priest came, bringing with him a bridle and a horseman.

Once again, at midnight that night, the wailing began in Okehampton, and the priest simply walked up to poor old Benjamin Gayer and said in Arabic: 'Benjamin Gayer, the time has come for you to depart the town of Okehampton.' To everybody's surprise, the moaning stopped and he replied, 'Now you have spoken I will be gone.' With that he was transformed into a jet black horse. The priest summoned the horseman to come forward and instructed him to put the bridle on the horse and mount it. When he had done this, the horseman was told to ride the horse straight to Cranmere Pool without stopping and without letting the horse look back. Once he drew closer to the pool he was to drive the horse into the pool and, just as he neared the bank, he had to undo the bridle and throw himself clear.

The horseman carried out these instructions successfully and Benjamin Gayer was plunged to the bottom of the pool. To make sure his spirit never returned, he was condemned to empty the water from the pool with a sieve.

For months Benjamin Gayer worked away, sieving water from the pool, until one day he spotted a dead sheep nearby. He skinned the sheep and lined his sieve, and so was able to empty the pool as requested. However, he did his job so quickly that the water from the pool flowed down and flooded Okehampton.

The residents were furious and so they made sure he could cause no more trouble; they had his spirit condemned to make trusses of sand, and this was to be carried out until the day of judgement.

Some say that you can still hear Benjamin wailing by Cranmere Pool on dark nights, although today it is no longer a pool but a marshy hollow.

MELDON

The Dartmoor Railway

Dartmoor Railway is a 15.5-mile stretch of railway line running across the northern edge of the moors between Meldon Quarry and Coleford Junction. The route was part of what was once the Southern Railway main line from London to North Cornwall and Plymouth. This stretch of the line was kept on to transport ballast from Meldon Quarry for use on the railways. When the quarry and the stretch of railway line were sold to Aggregate Industries, the concept of the Dartmoor Railway was created. The idea was for visitors to be able to reach the moors without a car.

Meldon Viaduct

Meldon Viaduct is a wonderful example of Victorian engineering. Spanning 341ft (165m), it is one of only two in the country of this type of construction. It was built in 1874 for the London & South Western Railway main line between Waterloo and Plymouth and was widened in 1878 to a double track. To widen the viaduct, a second viaduct was built alongside the first and, over the years, the two structures were tied together to reduce sway when trains crossed. The viaduct was closed to trains in the late 1960s. However, it was refurbished in 1996 and it is still a stunning feature of the Meldon landscape, providing a route for walkers and cyclists.

Meldon Pool

Meldon Pool is a flooded, disused limestone quarry which can be as deep as 39.5m. The limestone was quarried to fire the limestone kilns in the area.

An interesting but rather tragic story occurred in 1936 when a person from the area went missing and it was assumed that they had drowned in the pool – but no body was found.

It was decided that the old practice of 'singing the bones' would be tried, to see if the body could be discovered. 'Singing the bones' involved hymns and prayers being sung at the edge of the water where somebody had gone missing, in the hope that the body would emerge – the theory being that the sacred words would attract the lost soul, which would be released from limbo and so a Christian burial could be given. An Okehampton choir came and sang by the edge of Meldon and, although nothing happened immediately, incredibly, in a week's time, the body floated to the surface.

Meldon Pool is also known for the Meldon Bomb – where local youngsters plunge from 40ft high into the pool.

Meldon Lime kilns

There are two lime kilns at Meldon which have been restored by the Dartmoor National Park Authority. Years ago, local people met here as it was warm and some of the kilns even had bread ovens inside, which the women could bake their bread in. Apparently, tramps used to sleep around the kilns for warmth, and some even slept on the top edge for extra heat. Some stories tell of kiln-keepers coming to work in the mornings and finding charred corpses in the fire. It was thought that the vagrants had been overcome by the fumes and rolled in to their deaths. The lime kilns were also thought to have curative powers, and any child suffering from whooping cough could be cured by inhaling the fumes.

'Meldon Viaduct.' (Miles Wolstenholme)

'Lime Kiln, Meldon Quarries.' (Miles Wolstenholme)

'Meldon Reservoir.' (Miles Wolstenholme)

Meldon Quarry

Today quarrying continues, with Aggregate Industries extracting railway ballast, roadstone and other industrial aggregates, which are taken out by rail through Okehampton Station and on to the main line at Exeter.

Meldon Dam and Reservoir

A few hundred metres west along the trail from Meldon Viaduct is a turning, by a Sustrans mile-post, that gives access along a lane to Meldon Dam and Reservoir. The dam was built in 1972 in the West Okement Valley and has a span of 660ft (201m) and is 145ft high (45m). It is possible to walk around the reservoir using a permissive path, and access land to admire the views of the Dartmoor scenery.

Oxeye Daisy (*Leucanthemum vulgare*)

Known also as the dog daisy or moon daisy, this tall flower flourishes on roadside embankments and in fields. In the old days it was used in salves and medicines to cure several illnesses – including chest and liver diseases. The juice from the stem was also used to cure runny eyes.

Cross leaved Heath (*Erica tetralix*)

This evergreen plant looks like the bell heather which is also found on the moors However, cross leaved heath grows in the boggy areas and damp hollows, whilst bell heather prefers the drier heathland. Its branches spread and root themselves, and you will see it covering wide areas.

The Dunlin (*Calidris alpine*)

Dunlins are mainly found on the coast but a few pairs come to breed on Dartmoor on the high blanket bog. They keep their distance from humans and, if you do see one, it will probably be stooped over, probing in the ground for food. In fact, you can tell where a dunlin has been by the trail of marks it leaves in the ground where it has been looking for food. When it finds a fly or a worm, it'll swallow it in an instant, without stopping its probing.

Their nests are neat cups made of purple moor grass and bog cotton, built on a grass tussock on the boggy land. They usually lay four eggs. During the winter they head for the estuaries to probe and wade in the mud flats.

The Golden Plover (*Pluvialis apricaria*)

This wader is found on the high boggy moors. They dash along the ground in short spurts, pausing to pick up food which includes worms, slugs and seeds. In the summer, when they are breeding, you can sometimes hear their beautiful long call.

Their nests are sparsely constructed out of grass, and blend into the bog hummock or grass tussock. The female sits on the eggs whilst the male guards her, sounding the alarm and causing a diversion by pretending to be injured if the nest is approached. During the winter, golden plovers leave the moors for the lowland fields, flying in tight flocks.

Cosdon Hill

Cosdon Beacon or Cosdon Hill is a stunning mound of land that dominates the north of Dartmoor. Although it looks high, and was once thought to be the highest point on Dartmoor, at 550m it doesn't quite reach the peak of High Willhays at 621m.

Cosdon Hill was a very sacred place and is littered with ancient relics of archaeological and historical interest. There are nine Bronze Age settlements around the western side of Cosdon and two reaves. The two reaves on Cosdon appear to have defined a specific Bronze Age tribal territory.

Scattered over Cosdon you will find evidence of numerous cairns (around sixty-eight apparently), kistvaens, stone rows and what was once a stone circle. The most spectacular to see is the triple stone row which runs for about 150m and ends at a cairn, which is unusual in that it contains two kistvaens and would appear to be a 'his and hers' grave.

Lying in the shadow of Cosdon Beacon are four pretty villages, known as the Beacon Villages.

BELSTONE

Belstone is a tranquil village, a small cluster of houses surrounding a village green and overlooking the breathtaking slopes of the moor and the River Taw. There is a peaceful sleepiness about Belstone and you can imagine you are standing still in time.

Dartmoor ponies graze on the common in front of the pub, wandering occasionally into the village for the lusher grass of the village green. There are old stocks at the side of the road. Between the old Zion chapel and the stocks is a stone pound, now a garden maintained by the local WI. Stray animals used to be kept in here until their owners collected them.

St Mary's Church, built in the fifteenth century, towers over the pub with its graveyard backing right up to it. The Tors pub, a tall stone building, is very welcoming inside and is rumoured to be haunted by a White Lady.

The River Taw

Beginning its journey on the slopes of Hangingstone Hill, where the East Dart and West Okement also have their sources, the River Taw is considerably wider and faster by the time it passes below Belstone.

The Nine Maidens Stone Circle

If you walk out onto Belstone Common, on the way to Belstone Tor up Watchet Hill, and look carefully, you may come across a small, mysterious circle of seventeen stones, roughly 7m in diameter.

The circle is actually the remains of a Bronze Age barrow (the seventeen stones are part of the retaining wall of the burial chamber or kistvaen). Some of the stones have fallen and some have been removed, and it is said that you can never count the same number.

When the sun drops, a mysterious atmosphere hangs over the circle – maybe due to its lonely position, maybe due to the legend. If you happen to be there on a 'Hunter's Moon' then you might see the stones come back to life and take on their original form of nine dancing maidens.

It's wise to avoid visiting the circle during the pagan festivals as, on this site, a coven of witches gather to perform ritual ceremonies. A note for your diary – pagan festivals are:

- Yule – Winter solstice
- Imbolc – 31 January – 1 February
- Ostara – Spring equinox
- Beltane – 30 April – 1 May
- Litha – Midsummer solstice
- Lammas – 31 July – 1 August
- Mabon – Autumn equinox
- Samhain – 31 October – 1 November

The Hunter's Moon

The Hunter's Moon (also known as Blood Moon or Sanguine Moon) is the first full moon after the Harvest Moon, which is the full moon nearest to the autumn equinox. The Hunter's Moon and the Harvest Moon are special because there is no long period of darkness between the sunset and the moonrise for several days around these times. This was useful in the past as it meant that hunters could continue tracking their prey into the night, and farmers could continue harvesting as the moon rose – hence their names.

The Irishman's Wall

Back in the nineteenth century a group of sturdy Irishmen, employed by a land speculator who was attempting to enclose areas of the moor, undertook the task of building a straight stone wall up and over Belstone Tor. The wall was never finished as there was uproar from the locals, who pulled it down as fast as it was being built. Now it is so dilapidated in parts that it is hard to distinguish it from the surrounding stones.

Bogbean (*Menyanthes trifoliata*)

You will find bogbean growing in the wetter parts of bogs and in marshes, with its stems and leaves raised above the water's surface. Its roots spread under the water, causing it to colonise large stretches of marshland. It has very pretty white flowers, the petals of which are fringed with tiny pink hairs.

During the Middle Ages, bogbean was a cure for scurvy and the Irish believed it purified blood and got rid of boils. Extract of bogbean was recommended as a general health tonic. In the north of England, its leaves were used to flavour beer and were also dried and put in herbal cigarettes.

The White Willow (*Salix alba*)

The white willow is a medium to large-sized deciduous tree, growing up to 30m high with a trunk of up to 1m diameter. They grow in areas of moisture, especially along riverbanks. The wood has been traditionally used for basket making and sheep hurdles, and a hybrid of the white willow is grown specifically to make cricket bats.

White willow bark has medicinal properties and is used as a tincture to bring down fever, ease arthritis and relieve hay fever. It has analgesic properties.

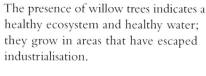
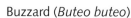

The presence of willow trees indicates a healthy ecosystem and healthy water; they grow in areas that have escaped industrialisation.

Buzzard (*Buteo buteo*)

You will often hear the haunting cry of a buzzard gliding effortlessly overhead. Circling on the warm thermals, he scours the moor with his keen eyes, searching for prey. Buzzards are larger than other birds of prey on Dartmoor and have white or light markings under their wings. They mainly eat rabbits but are willing to eat other small mammals.

Sticklepath. (Author's collection)

STICKLEPATH

Sticklepath is a small Dartmoor village that evolved along the old ridgeway path between Exeter and Launceston (once the capital of Cornwall). It is unusual in that it didn't develop around a Manor House or a rectory. The chapel was built in 1147 and the village appears to have evolved around farming and milling. The first grain mill was built in 1294 (where the Finch Foundry Museum is today) and several other mills were established on the stream running into the Taw.

The Finch Foundry, now owned by the National Trust, is a nineteenth-century water-powered foundry which is open to the public. It is still in working order and there are regular demonstrations for visitors.

Sticklepath is also along the route of the Tarka Trail, a 30-mile trail that follows the old railway tracks of North Devon and is now available to cyclists. It runs between Braunton and Meeth.

There are two pubs in Sticklepath, the Taw River Inn and the Devonshire Arms.

SOUTH ZEAL

South Zeal, like Sticklepath, does not have its own church – just a chapel in the centre of the village. The church is situated in South Tawton which, in the old days, was a manor, with South Zeal being a village in the manor. The village has a manor hall, hence its name (Zeal comes from the old word 'zele', meaning 'hall').

The main business in South Zeal was spinning and weaving, the wool trade being the most valuable Devon industry up until the eighteenth century.

During the nineteenth century, South Zeal housed many migrant workers from Ireland. They came to work in the important Ramsley copper mine on the hill above. The influx of Irish workers caused the village to be known locally as the Irishman's Town. During this time South Zeal had a baker, a shoemaker, a tailor and a milliner, plus a range of general stores and a pub. Today there is a general store and two pubs.

The Oxenham Arms is a beautiful looking pub with a fascinating history. Originally built in the twelfth century and then rebuilt in the sixteenth century, it has been a dower house for both the Burgoynes and the Oxenhams. Just before the death of one of the Oxenham family, it is said that a white bird appears in the pub. Built into an interior wall is an ancient menhir.

The Kings Arms is an ancient cider house and still a hub of the village. It hosts many events during the year and is one of the venues of the Dartmoor Folk Festival.

The Dartmoor Folk Festival

A traditional, friendly festival open to everyone, every August the Dartmoor Folk Festival attracts some of the top national and local artists to South Zeal. It is a weekend event offering live music, workshops and concerts, with camping in nearby fields for those wishing to stay.

SOUTH TAWTON

South Tawton, another of the Beacon villages, is an ancient demesne (royal manor) dating back to the time of the Saxons, if not the Romans. It is located on the banks of the River Taw and was mentioned in the Domesday Book. St Andrew's Church, a fifteenth-century granite structure with a wonderful interior including a tinners' rabbit, contains many plaques and memorials to local people, including the Oxenham family who held a large estate nearby during the eighteenth century.

South Tawton Church House is a stunning, two-storey thatched building which has been lovingly restored. It is used today for events and functions and is worth a look around.

THROWLEIGH

The parish of Throwleigh is tucked away down the pretty lanes of Dartmoor, with the Bronze Age hut circles at Shilstone Tor being the earliest visible remains of inhabitants in the area. Throwleigh is still predominantly a farming community and so the population is spread out. The parish now includes Wonson, Murchington and Providence.

The picturesque Northmore Arms claims to be the most authentic English pub in the world, with no pool table and no jukebox - just a few board games, a great cosy atmosphere, real ale and good food.

Tinners' Rabbits

The church at Throwleigh has an example of a tinners' rabbit – an engraving of three animals; usually they look like hares or rabbits but they only have three ears between them. They are found on medieval roof bosses in several churches on Dartmoor. The sign may have evolved from an ancient fertility symbol but is also seen as a sign of the Holy Trinity.

White Moor Down Stone Circle

This stunning stone circle stands in a very desolate part of the moor. If you walk here from the north and across Cosdon Hill, then take care. The path skirts around the edge of Raybarrow Pool, a dangerous bog, and is not easy to navigate when it has been raining.

The circle was restored in 1896 as many of the stones had previously been removed. Now there are eighteen stones standing or leaning. It is believed that the circle would originally have consisted of nineteen stones.

THE TEIGN VALLEY

The River Teign begins its journey high on the moor. It has two main sources – the North Teign, which starts high on the moor, and the South Teign, which starts just to the west of Fernworthy

'Teignhead Clapper.' (Miles Wolstenholme)

Forest near the Grey Wethers stone circle and is the location of the legend attached to the stone circle (*see* p.123). Joining each other just beyond Gidleigh, the rivers form the River Teign and flow for around 30 miles over the edge of Dartmoor and on to Teignmouth.

The route can be walked from various points and is a very pretty and interesting journey.

CHAGFORD

Chagford developed in the 1300s as a stannary town along with Plympton, Ashburton and Tavistock. The Dartmoor tinners used to send their ingots to the nearest stannary town by pack-horse. The stannary officials and tin dealers would gather there to examine and buy the tin. Wool was once important to Chagford too. From 1800 to 1848 a wool factory was in operation, making blankets from the local sheep wool.

Today, Chagford is a popular and flourishing market town with a slightly alternative, arty population; a great place to stay whilst visiting Dartmoor. Two overflowing hardware shops can be found in the centre, along with several good-quality cafés and restaurants and some interesting shops.

St Michael's Church

A beautiful church which hosts many concerts. In the churchyard is an unusual Roman altar. It was dug up in the 1860s and could quite possibly have been the altar of an earlier church.

Shootings at the Three Crowns

Opposite the church is a very old pub which was built in the thirteenth century as a Manor House. A couple of people have been shot here. In 1641, a lady called Mary Whyddon was shot whilst standing in the doorway. Apparently, the man who shot her had taken a fancy to her but she had rejected him – much to her misfortune. Two years later, a man named Sidney Godolphin was hit by a musket shot and died in the house.

Chagford Town Centre. (Author's collection)

Outside of Chagford, heading towards the moors, are some very interesting and mysterious ancient sites. Scorhill stone circle is a wonderfully atmospheric stone circle – well worth finding. Drive out through Murchington and Gidleigh; the stone circle is then a short walk from the small car park. The path is well worn, so easy to follow across the moorland.

It is unclear what these ancient circles were for. Fires were built within the circle of stones, and the way the stones are laid out suggests that they were used for some kind of sun worship. There are thirty stones altogether; twenty-three are still standing. One legend claims that if a local woman was accused of being unfaithful, she was forced to kneel before a stone and pray for forgiveness. If she was forgiven the stone stayed upright, if she was found guilty then the stone would fall and crush her to death. Consequently, under each fallen stone there is said to be a female skeleton.

Some people believe that ancient sun worshippers would sacrifice humans here, whilst others believe that a giant troll lives in the area, who catches unsuspecting sheep and brings them back to the circle to cook. There is often a fire seen flickering in the centre.

Fernworthy Forest and Fernworthy Stone Circle

During the First World War, the government realised that Britain was overly dependent on imported timber supplies. This led to the development of the Forestry Commission in 1919, which was given a target to plant 1,700,000 acres of timber by 1980. In their search for land, the Forestry Commission persuaded the Prince of Wales to allow them to plant 5,000 acres of woodland on Dartmoor. One of the first areas to be forested was Fernworthy, and by 1930, 800 acres of trees had been planted. This is Fernworthy Forest.

Unfortunately, the forest was planted on an area with plenty of archaeological features, one of which was Fernworthy stone circle. But fortunately, the Forestry Commission left a clearing around the circle so it can be found today. The circle dates from the Bronze Age and there is confusion as to how many stones there actually are in the circle. Some say twenty-six, some

'Scorhill Shadows.' (Miles Wolstenholme)

twenty-seven, and one count included the two lying down stones and so counted twenty-nine. Once again there is speculation as to the reason for the circle. A dig in 1890 led to the discovery of charcoal, suggesting the use of fire.

If you make it to the other side onto the open moors you will, after a bit of a search, come across two wonderful stone circles forming a figure of eight called Grey Wethers. 'Wether' is another term for sheep. It is said that, from a distance, the two stone circles look like a flock of sheep grazing.

The Legend of Grey Wethers

Story has it that one summer, many years ago, three peasants were cutting peat on the moors near the stone circles. One of the men, Varnes, lived permanently on Dartmoor and one night he told the other two the story of an evil place – the Grey Wethers:

> Hundreds of years ago, a peasant called Zorac came here to live. He was from a tribe of people who worshipped Belus, the Sun God. Very quickly he grew rich, as he was very faithful to Belus. However, even sun worshippers can become greedy and, one midsummer, he decided that rather than offer one of his own healthy sheep for sacrifice to Belus, he would steal one from his neighbour. Well, Belus was not to be fooled and, knowing what Zorac had done, he decided to punish him. That night Zorac returned to where he had left his flock to find two stone circles in their place.
>
> To this day the stone circles stand there. However, every Midsummer Night they turn back into sheep and graze from midnight until sunrise. Legend has it that if any man shears one of the sheep and sprinkles the fleece with water from the rock basin on top of Kestor, the fleece will turn to gold. The fleece needs to be sheared using the shears of Zorac, which are buried with him. They are useless until they have been dipped in the River Teign at midnight and they must be held in the water until a tress of hair appears. This is to be used to catch the sheep.

'Grey Wethers.' (Miles Wolstenholme)

Well, upon hearing this legend, Lynhur, one of the peat cutters, became obsessed by the thought of a golden fleece and how he would be rich for life. At Midsummer's Eve he went out in search of Zorac's burial place and there, just as the legend said, he discovered a stone coffin. Inside he found the skeleton of Zorac and a pair of rusty shears. He took the shears and headed towards the River Teign, filling his flask with some water from the top of Kestor as he went by.

When he reached the river, he dipped the shears into the water. As he did so a voice rang out in the dark of night. 'Strike! strike! Crimson blood shall stain the flood and whet the glistening blade that shears the sheep.' In terror, Lynhur pulled the shears back out – but then he remembered that he needed a tress of hair to appear. He plunged the shears back into the water, which immediately turned blood red, and the voice sounded again. 'Strike! Strike! See there before thee in the stream, to bind the sheep, fair tresses gleam.' He grabbed at the tresses but was too slow and only managed to pull out part of them.

Excited but terrified, he raced up to the stones and sat down, waiting for them to turn into sheep. But he fell asleep and, when he awoke, it was a few hours past midnight already. In a panic he tried to capture a sheep, but because he only had a thin tress of hair it took him a while, and, when he started to shear the sheep, it took him forever as the shears were not as sharp as they needed to be. Terrified, Lynhur realised that the sky was beginning to lighten as morning approached. He cursed himself, the water, the shears and the tress, and wished he had never started, as a sense of doom came upon him. Looking up he saw that the sheep in the herd had grown huge and were surrounding him. Suddenly a voice rang out, 'Thou that seekest to gain the treasure of the dead, shall win the fatal gift the grave doth yield instead.'

The next day, Lynhur was found dead beneath one of the stones which had fallen on him.

Fly Agaric (*Amanita muscaria*)

Well known from children's story books, these pretty toadstools live in the woodlands of Dartmoor and look magical with their red caps and white flecks. The first recorded appearance of the fly agaric is in a 1261 fresco in France; its common name stems from the thirteenth century, when it was discovered that if you broke it up and soaked it in milk, it would attract and kill flies.

Don't touch this toadstool, it is poisonous! It is also known for its hallucinogenic effects, and in folklore is reputed to induce erotic energy, prophetic sight and incredible muscular strength.

Round Leaved Sundew (*Drosera rotundifolia*)

This bogland plant is carnivorous, feeding on insects which are attracted to its bright red colour and get caught on its sticky hairs. It evolved into a carnivore due to the lack of nutrients in its habitat; it uses enzymes to dissolve the insects and extract the goodness from them.

In the Middle Ages, sundew was believed to help cure corns and was later discovered to contain antibiotics.

Spinsters Rock

Spinsters Rock is a Neolithic chambered tomb. Originally, the stones would have been covered with a long mound of earth or stones. It has been suggested that chambered tombs were either for funeral use, for use as territorial markers, or even as status symbols. It is obvious that the construction could only take place as a communal activity, involving teamwork, which suggests a high level of social organisation within the community.

'Fly Agaric.' (Miles Wolstenholme)

'Spinsters Rock.' (Miles Wolstenholme)

DREWSTEIGNTON

A quiet village with under 600 inhabitants, Drewsteignton looks down onto the Teign Gorge. There are several places of interest for visitors – the old pub the Drewe Arms, Prestonbury Castle and the not-to-be-missed Castle Drogo.

The Drewe Arms is famed for having the longest-serving and oldest landlady a pub has known. Aunt Mabel, or Mrs Mudge, lived and served behind the bar until the ripe old age of 101. The pub is still full of character and charm.

Prestonbury Castle

Prestonbury Castle is one of the most well known Iron Age hill forts on Dartmoor. It is just outside of Drewsteignton and is a 3-acre encampment enclosed by a concentric arrangement of banks and ditches, which would have been much higher and deeper than they are now.

Castle Drogo

Castle Drogo was the last castle to be built in England. Julius Drewe commissioned its design by leading architect of the time Edwin Lutyens. Building started in 1911 but, due to the First World War and the economic downturn, the property wasn't completed until 1930 and was much smaller than originally planned. It was the last private residence in England to be built entirely of granite, using styles of castle building from medieval and Tudor times. Its defensive features are purely decorative as the private home was never used as a 'castle'. Its austere external appearance hides the cosy family interior, which was lit with electricity supplied from two turbines in the River Teign below. The castle was given to the National Trust along with 600 acres of grounds, and is now open to the public. A wonderful place to visit.

Fingle Bridge

Fingle is the name of a stream that rises on Whiddon Down and joins the River Teign at Fingle Bridge – hence its name. The bridge was built in the early 1660s to service local industries, which at the time consisted of corn milling, charcoal burning, bark ripping and timber supply. Packhorses were used to transport the products and that is why the bridge was so narrow. The triangular recesses were built for pedestrians to step into whilst a packhorse passed by.

Originally there was a corn mill below the bridge, but this burnt down in the 1890s and was never rebuilt. Before it burnt down it had started to serve refreshments to passing travellers. After the fire, the nearest cottage was persuaded to carry on serving refreshments, and eventually a tea shed was built. Over time this has been rebuilt and extended, and is now the Anglers Rest.

DUNSFORD

Just off the B3212, the main road from Exeter to Moretonhampstead, lies Dunsford, a peaceful and pretty village nestled in the Teign Valley. There doesn't appear to be much written about the history of Dunsford, but it was mentioned in the Domesday Book in 1086 and there has been a church there since before 1260 on the same site as the existing church, St Mary's, which was built in 1430. Dunsford also has a chapel, which can be found on the main B3212 near Steps Bridge. This was built in 1885.

The village today has a thriving community with a primary school, village shop and post office, tea room and pub.

One of the best-known features of Dunsford is the Fulford family, one of the oldest families in Devon. They can be traced back to the twelfth-century William de Fulford, who was granted the estate by Richard of England for going on crusade. The family still occupy the same 3,000-acre estate just outside of Dunsford. The present house dates back to the sixteenth century and Francis Fulford and his family live there now. They are probably best known for the documentary-style television series *The F***ing Fulfords*.

The Dunsford Show

The Dunsford Show takes place every summer and has done for generations. It is a traditional village show at its best, with live music, a horse show, a dog show, children's entertainment, a beer tent, dancing and lots more.

'Fingle Bridge.' (Miles Wolstenholme)

Dunsford. (Author's collection)

The Dunsford Nature Reserve

Approaching Dartmoor on the main road from Dunsford, you will come across Steps Bridge. Here is a popular entrance to the footpath through the Dunsford Nature Reserve, 57 hectares of river valley woodland, heath-covered rocky slopes, and fertile floodplain scrub and grassland. The footpath follows the River Teign in the direction of Drewsteignton and Castle Drogo. The nature reserve is well known for its wild narcissus (abundant in spring) and fritillary butterfly.

Blackingstone Rock

Blackingstone Rock is said to be the highest tor outcrop on Dartmoor, at 75ft. This makes it a popular destination for climbers. The views from the top of the tor are far reaching in all directions on a clear day and, for those of you who don't have crampons and ropes, there is a flight of steps cut into the eastern side with a handrail. On the top of the tor you will see many rock basins, which are usually filled with rain water. There is much debate as to how these basins came about.

But how did Blackingstone Rock itself come to be here, so far from the other tors – with not another rock outcrop in sight? William Crossing suggests that it appeared long ago when, one day, the Devil and King Arthur were having a disagreement. King Arthur took his stand on the hill where Blackingstone Rock is today and the Devil ensconced himself on the hill where Hel Tor is. They decided to settle the dispute using physical strength and hurl quoits at each other. Without a second thought the battle started, and as the quoits hit the ground they turned to stone, forming what are now called Hel Tor and Blackingstone Rock. They are 1.2 miles apart from each other.

Blackthorn (*Prunus spinosa*)

A large shrub, and occasionally a small tree, blackthorn can be found on the edge of woodland thickets or in hedges around the lower lands of Dartmoor. It is thick and thorny and provides a protected place in which birds can nest.

The fruits are called sloes and are used to make sloe gin. They can also be used to make jam and wine. It is thought that the blackthorn may be related to the damson and other domestic plums. In the Middle Ages, the green sloes were used as a purgative for colic.

The wood of the blackthorn is hard and tough, and its main use is for the teeth of hay rakes and for walking sticks. It is also used traditionally to make the Irish cudgel (a club).

Pied Flycatcher (*Ficedula hypoleuca*)

Found in the mature woodlands of Dartmoor, this little bird can often be seen on the lookout for caterpillars and insects. It darts off to catch its prey, often taking it to the ground. The male is black on top with a white wing patch and white spot above its bill; the female is grey-brown on its back and doesn't have the white spot. They nest in holes in dead trees, the female building the nest and lining it with animal hair, wool and feathers. In October they fly to Africa for the winter, returning back to Dartmoor in April to breed.

BRIDFORD

Tucked away high on the slopes of the valley is the small village of Bridford, with its population today of around 560 people. The earliest evidence of human occupation is a collection of flints found on Hedgemoor Farm, dating back to the Mesolithic period.

Bridford Manor was recorded in the Domesday Book as belonging to Joel de Totneis, and subsequently passed through the hands of various Lords of the Manor, including the Valletorts, Champernownes and Sir Simon Leach of Modbury, until, by the late eighteenth century, it was owned by Sir Robert Palk, who lived at Haldon House. The local population were employed in farming or in the local mines.

The church dates back to the thirteenth century and was dedicated to St Thomas Becket in 1259. A couple of points of interest are the tinners' rabbit on a roof boss in the centre of the nave, the rood screen dating back to 1508, and the large fourteenth-century demi figures on the north side of the parclose screen.

The traditional and cosy pub in the village is called the Bridford Inn and dates back to the seventeenth century.

Peregrine Falcon (*Falco peregrinus*)

This falcon is large and powerful, with long broad wings and a short tail. It has a blue-grey back with a white face and white-speckled breast, and a black moustache. Peregrine falcons are found around rocky cliff edges and uplands, and have been spotted around quarries and some rocky outcrops of Dartmoor. They nest on rocky ledges, sometimes scraping a depression out of the loose earth.

Agile hunters, they plunge to their prey, wings folded back, at high speeds. The blow from the talons will instantly break the neck or back of prey – usually a flying pigeon or grouse.

The peregrine wasn't popular during the war, as it would often intercept carrier pigeons; hunting it was therefore encouraged. Today, it is protected because its numbers have dropped due to the chemical build-up in its prey from the pesticides used in farming.

Holly (*Ilex aquifolium*)

Native to the UK, the holly grows everywhere except on wet soils. It is commonly used for hedges as it can be trimmed.

The holly has long been a symbol of Christmas, and years ago it was believed to be unlucky to chop down a holly tree – that is why so many are still found today in ancient hedgerows. It was also said that the holly had the power to ward off evil, and a good year for holly berries meant that a hard winter would follow. In reality, a good crop of berries meant a fine summer had just passed.

CHRISTOW

The earliest signs of human occupation in Christow are the Bronze Age hut circles on the high slopes of Christow Common and the occasional find of a worked flint, or the remaining chippings from where the flint was worked. This evidence dates back to the end of the New Stone Age/early Bronze Age.

It is not known exactly when Christow village developed and there is no record of it in the Domesday Book. Its name derives from Saxon times, 'stow' being Old English for 'a holy place'.

In 1332 it was recorded as being part of Cowick, and thirty-seven names were recorded in Christow, seeming to reflect the farm or place name of the inhabitant. William de Christouwe clearly lived in Christow, Roger Clampytte more than likely lived at Clampitt, and William de Alre was probably from Aller Farm.

In 1451, the manor of Christow passed to Tavistock Abbey and, after the Dissolution of the Monasteries, into the ownership of the Russell family, soon to be the Dukes of Bedford (*see* p.93). The community at this time was a farming community, and many of the farmhouses date back to the fifteenth and sixteenth centuries.

During the nineteenth century the first mines were opened. There were lodes of manganese, copper, lead, silver, zinc and iron within Christow, and thousands of tons of ore were produced. Another industry at this time was the quarrying of hard blue rock at Scattor. After the rock had been crushed at the quarry it was transported to Christow Station by an overhead railway.

In 1850 various trades were recorded in the area, as well as seventeen farms. There were two shopkeepers (one of whom was also the cattle doctor), a blacksmith, a shoemaker, a stone mason and a tailor. The mill and its complex of cottages was used either for grain or for fulling (cloth trade), and later became a slaughterhouse. Other trades listed were saddlery and woodcutting.

The Teign Valley Line

Opened in 1882 by the Great Western Railway, this line ran between Newton Abbot and Ashton on the other side of the Teign Valley, until 1904 when it was connected to Exeter. A station at Christow was built with goods sidings to load the wagons with stone and ore from the local quarries.

In 1903, the Teign Valley Railway was operating both a goods and passenger service. When the car arrived, the quarries and railway were busy. However, after the war, when car ownership increased, the quarries closed and along with them the railway ceased to operate.

St James' Church

As is the case with most Dartmoor churches, the present church of Christow was built on the site of an Anglo-Saxon church, of which there is no remaining evidence as these churches were wooden. A Norman church would have replaced the Saxon building, and the only physical evidence remaining is the large, square Norman font inside.

The present building was constructed during the fifteenth century; the swords carved on its pinnacles are symbolic of the martyrdom of St James, to whom the church was dedicated. In 1785 the peal of bells was increased from four to six, although it now has eight which are rung regularly by an enthusiastic local bell-ringing group.

Ramsons (*Allium ursinum*)

Carpeting the steep woody banks of the Teign Valley during spring, beside the B3193, this member of the garlic family gives off a pungent odour and its strong flavour will impart to the milk of any cows that eat it. You can chop and cook the leaves and use them to flavour sauces and food; it is also thought to cure digestive problems.

Eurasian Badger (*Meles meles*)

Badgers live in deciduous woods near cultivated land. They are very shy and you are more likely to see one dead on the road than alive in its habitat. Dark grey, with black and white striped faces, they are nocturnal animals foraging around on the woodland floors for worms. They eat insects and small mammals and have been known to break open a bees' nest in search of the honey.

Badgers live in groups of between four and twelve adults, in a hole in the ground called a sett. A sett has several interconnecting passages with resting chambers and separate nests inside; a heap of soil, old bedding and hairs outside a sett means it is still in use. Sometimes a sett will be used for hundreds of years.

Badgers can be fierce with a powerful bite, and will protect their young at all costs. They usually have two to three cubs per year in February, which stay underground for the first eight weeks being nursed by their mothers. They feed all spring and summer, then are ready to face their first winter.

Badgers can live for about fifteen years, but most die young at about three years.

Canonteign

Canonteign Manor derives its name from the canons of St Mary du Val in Normandy, who are recorded as owning the manor of Teigne in the Domesday Book, along with the name of the manor, 'Teigne'. In 1268, the manor passed to the Priory of Merton in Surrey and was at this time known as Canonteign.

In 1542 the Manor House was sold to Robert Davy, a wealthy merchant from Crediton who paid £200 for the house and lands, which included 'the grain and fulling mills at Kennick and at Christow village'. Fulling mills were used in the production of cloth at the cleaning stage, when the fast-flowing water was used.

In 1812 Lady Pellow, wife of Sir Edward Pellow, purchased the house along with the manors of Christow and Canonteign. Edward Pellow was a British Naval Officer who was knighted in 1793 for personal courage and tactical brilliance. He never lived at the house as he preferred to be by the sea in his house at Teignmouth. He was made a baron in 1814 and took the title Lord Exmouth of Canonteign. He was then made a viscount in 1816 and, when he retired in 1816, decided to take residence at Canonteign. However, the house was too old and run-down for him to live in so he built a new Georgian mansion to the west. The old Manor House became the estate bailiff's home and was later divided into a farmhouse and two cottages for the estate workers' families. Today the Manor House is a residential dwelling.

The new Canonteign House was owned and lived in by the viscount's ancestors and went through many changes. Today, Canonteign Estate is a venue for weddings and corporate events, plus a popular visitor attraction with its stunning waterfall, the Canonteign Falls.

HENNOCK

A small and peaceful village high in the hills above the Teign Valley, with stunning views back over the valley, Hennock has a few old buildings of interest to look at.

The thatched village hall was originally a barn built by the White Canons of Torre Abbey to store the tithes collected from the landowners and farms in the area. It was used as a tithe barn until the Dissolution of the Monasteries, when it passed to the vicar of the local church. Since then it has been used as a shippon for cattle, stables, and a coach house and store. After the First World War, returning local servicemen pooled their money and bought the barn between them. They converted it to a village hall to be used by the community, and it still is today.

St Mary's Church

The existing church was built on the site of an Anglo-Saxon church, which was replaced by a Norman building. The font inside dates back to 1170; the tower possibly dates back to 1250. The rest of the building was constructed around 1450, and the rood screen and decorated ceiling above it are from this period too. At the gateway to the churchyard you will see a memorial tablet dating back to 1603.

The Reservoirs

The three reservoirs of Kennick, Tottiford and Trenchford can be reached from Christow and Hennock, and are a popular walking destination for many locals and visitors alike. There is a car park and picnic tables here, and the reservoirs are promoted to attract visitors. Trenchford Reservoir offers pike fishing, whilst Kennick is a top rainbow trout fishery.

Tottiford was the first reservoir to be built on Dartmoor, in 1861, and covers 31 acres. Kennick was dammed in 1884 and covers 52 acres, and the Trenchford Reservoir was dammed in 1907 and covers 30 acres.

In November 2009, South West Water drained the water in Tottiford in order to carry out some maintenance and, much to everybody's astonishment, at the bottom in the mud was a Bronze Age ritual site. In 1861 no records of ancient sites were kept and therefore nobody knew of the existence of this complex under the water. It is one of the most important discoveries of recent times on Dartmoor, and it is interesting to note that this area of the moor contains relatively few prehistoric remains.

This complex dates back to the early Bronze Age and includes a double stone row and single row, ending at burial cairns, a 22m-diameter stone circle and at least eight other cairns. Some flint tools were also discovered, including knives and piercing tools, notched blades and arrowheads, dating back to Mesolithic times – around 8,000 years ago.

Lizard (*Lacerta vivipara*)

Between 10-15cm long, with a brown or grey-brown body covered with darker patches, the lizard can often be seen basking in the sun on a rock or log. It relies on external heat to maintain its body temperature. The lizard eats insects and spiders and its young are born alive and not hatched from eggs. These too are fed on insects and spiders.

CENTRAL DARTMOOR

PRINCETOWN

Driving into Princetown, you will be struck by the strange, empty feeling. There are no busy shops, there is no hustle and bustle of daily life, and few people or cars pass by. Maybe it's because of its location in the middle of the remote moor, or maybe it's because there is a large, forbidding prison situated here. The people you are most likely to spot are tourists, setting off to walk or cycle along the disused railway track from the car park in the centre of town, or visiting the fascinating and informative Dartmoor National Park Visitors' Centre.

Princetown was established in 1785 by Sir Thomas Tyrwhitt, who was then the Prince of Wales' private secretary. He called it Prince's Town. His intention was to develop the moorland for farming and create an agricultural community. These plans were unsuccessful as Dartmoor's harsh climate and infertile soil made it nearly impossible to grow crops.

The war with France in 1803 gave Tyrwhitt another idea. Britain had taken so many prisoners that the prisons were bursting, and prisoners were being kept in wretched conditions in the hulls of disused boats in Plymouth. Tyrwhitt persuaded the authorities to build a prison in Prince's Town, an ideal location due to its remoteness and its proximity to the coast, where many prisoners were brought in. The prison brought many jobs and trade to the town. It was the prisoners who built the church.

In 1823, the first iron railway was opened – The Plymouth & Dartmoor Railway. It was extended to Princetown in 1827, bringing provisions for the farmers and local residents. It was also used to transport granite from the nearby quarries to the docks at Plymouth. By 1840 the railway was closed.

Dartmoor Prison

Opened in 1809, Dartmoor Prison originally consisted of five granite prison blocks enclosed by two high circular walls. Each prison block was three-storeys high with 2ft square windows. There was no glass in the windows. The first two floors were cold, draughty open dormitories, with hammocks for the inmates hanging between rows of iron posts. Each dormitory contained 500 men, but it wasn't long before 750 men were crammed in as more and more prisoners arrived. Two more blocks had to be built in 1811.

The prison housed both French and then American prisoners of war and was finally left empty in 1816 for thirty-four years. Today, three of the original French prison blocks remain.

'HMP Princetown.' (Miles Wolstenholme)

Deaths

Between 1809 and 1815, around 1,500 prisoners died – mostly from diseases such as smallpox, typhus and pneumonia caused by the bad conditions, but also through fights and whilst attempting to escape. There were also some suicides.

The bodies were buried outside the walls in cheap wooden coffins or wrapped in shrouds. Fifty years later, the harsh weather eventually revealed the bones of these poor men and the governor of the convict prison had them collected and divided into two piles, one French, one American. These were then buried in separate cemeteries behind the prison with an obelisk to identify each nationality. Today the obelisks are well-tended. The Americans have identified who died at the prison and erected two plaques in their memory.

Convicts

In 1850 the prison was reopened and used for British convicts. The convicts converted the dormitory blocks into individual cells which were dark and unventilated. Before long, many of Britain's worst criminals were imprisoned here as its location made it a very safe prison. The convicts had to work on the moor, digging the bogs to drain them and make the soil suitable for cultivation, and quarrying granite with hammers.

Escapes

Of course, hundreds of prisoners tried to escape. Most commonly they tried to make a run for it whilst working on the moors when the mist was thick. Some of the French and Americans bribed the prison guards, who would give them a hand over the wall or happen to look the other way as someone escaped. The most popular means of escape were:

- Making a run for it when working out on the moor
- Digging tunnels through the floors
- Hacking through the barred windows then climbing to the ground using ropes made of anything available
- Digging the stones out of the cell walls to make a hole

The Conscientious Objectors

In 1917, during the First World War, men stopped volunteering to go to war as stories were heard of the conditions. It was then made mandatory for men to go to war. The conchies (conscientious objectors) were the men who refused to be conscripted because they believed it was wrong to kill. This type of feeling wasn't allowed in those days, and so they were tried and made to spend the rest of the war in prisons or 'work settlements'. Dartmoor Prison was renamed as a work settlement and housed 1,100 objectors. Prison staff and locals considered the objectors to be cowards. In 1918 they were released.

Riot in the Prison

On 24 January 1932 a major riot broke out in the prison. Around 200 prisoners went on a rampage after breakfast, setting fire to the governor's office and destroying records. The chapel and some other buildings were smashed up and the riot ended with many injuries as the police and soldiers were brought in to calm the situation down.

Today

Although the prison has traditionally housed high security prisoners, it was downgraded to a Category C prison in 2001, as permission was withheld by the local council for alterations to improve security. It now holds 645 Category C and D prisoners.

The category of a prisoner is directly related to an individual's escape potential:

- Category A: those who have the support and means for escape, or present a threat to the public. Usually these prisoners are kept in 'high security' prisons
- Category B: those who are a high escape risk but do not have the means
- Category C: those who are not a high escape risk but may be opportunists
- Category D: those who represent no risk either of escaping or being a threat to the public

Soldiers Three

There is a legend that originated from the prison of a convict who managed to escape whilst out working on the moor. He set off for Plymouth but was soon lost in a thick, dark mist, silencing everything around him. He began to despair and, when he had reached his lowest and was wishing to be recaptured, he saw three soldiers marching towards him in old-fashioned army uniforms. He felt a strange urge to walk with them and joined them in their march, not knowing where they came from or where they were going. Feeling calm now, he marched with them until suddenly he heard a shout. Somebody was calling his name. He was found.

None of the search party who found him saw the other soldiers, and they didn't believe his story, but one of the warders later remembered that there was a plaque in Princetown church in memory of three soldiers who, during the war, had lost their way in a blizzard whilst marching from Plymouth to Princetown. Their bodies were found at the same spot where the searchers had found the escaped convict.

Snipe (*Gallinago gallinago*)

This medium-sized wading bird has short legs and an extraordinarily long bill. Measuring a quarter of the length of its body, the bill has a flexible and highly sensitive tip which enables it to detect and identify its food. It usually digs for its food, which consists of worms and other invertebrates, but it also eats insects from the surface. The snipe is dark, with contrasting light stripes on its crown and back, and its tail is fringed with reddish-brown and white.

Dartmoor's snipe population constitutes one of the largest left in southern England. Their nests are built on the ground and are well hidden, and a clutch of four pale greenish-brown eggs is laid every year.

The Whiteworks Tin Mines

The remains of one of the largest tin mines on Dartmoor can be found just outside of Princetown. It was operational between 1820 and 1825 and was last worked in 1876. Today, only ruined walls and old shafts can be seen – evidence of the workers' homes, which were precariously close to Fox Tor Mire.

Fox Tor Mire

In a valley to the south-west of Princetown is a large boggy area into which several small rivers flow. This is known as Fox Tor Mire and is reputedly the most dangerous bog on Dartmoor. It is a place where people and animals are sucked to their death, according to legends and stories. Some say that this was the inspiration for Sir Arthur Conan Doyle's Grimpen Mire and, if you are a Sherlock Holmes fan, you will have heard of Fox Tor Mire already.

Bog Asphodel (*Narthecium ossifragum*)

Bog asphodel likes wet ground, and here it will send out thick underground stems which spread easily and form large patches. In July it produces a fragrant yellow flower, and in autumn its fruit capsules develop and contain pale yellow seeds, with a tail at each end to help the seed float in times of flooding.

'Ossifragum' means 'bone-breaking' and the plant was given this name because it was believed that it caused brittle bones in sheep that ate it. This was proved to be untrue, and an absence of mineral salts in the soils most probably caused the ailment.

Heron (*Ardea cinerea*)

A large, long-legged and long-necked bird with a white head and black-streaked neck, the heron is most often spotted standing still and alert beside water, waiting for a fish to swim within striking distance. When it spots one, it strikes with its long, sharp bill and swallows the fish whole. As well as fish, a heron will eat frogs, reptiles, insects, small mammals and even birds.

Herons build large nests in colonies in the tops of tall trees and bushes. The nest is built of sticks and twigs, with a hollow in the top; the same nest is used again and again, growing each year until some reach several feet across.

The females lay three to five eggs and, when they hatch, both parents feed them by regurgitating their food.

The UK heron population falls after severe winters, when the frozen rivers and lakes deprive the birds of food.

Childe's Tomb

On the edge of Fox Tor Mire stands a relatively modern cross on a base of large stone blocks, over a prehistoric burial site. It has clearly replaced an older cross. The name of the cross derives from what is probably the best-known legend of Dartmoor, Childe the Hunter of Plymstock.

Childe the Hunter

Childe was a rich man living in and owning much of the land in Plymstock. One of his favourite pastimes was to hunt on Dartmoor and he spent as much time as he could out there, never afraid of being alone. One day he was out with his horse, as usual, when without warning a snowstorm came upon them, thick and fast, covering their tracks and causing them to lose their way. Childe tried to carry on through the snow for a while, but soon became exhausted and thought it better to rest until the storm passed. The storm carried on – relentless, thick, fast and cold, freezing Childe to his bones. After hours of this he became desperate and, in a last attempt to keep warm, he killed his poor horse, pulled out its innards and climbed inside.

Weeks later, the two bodies were found and Childe's death was reported to the monks of Tavistock Abbey. Childe's will stated that all his lands would pass to the church wherever he was buried and so the monks of Tavistock agreed that the Abbey Church was the best place to lay him to rest.

When the monks at Plymstock Abbey got wind of this there was uproar. As far as they were concerned, Childe's land ought to belong to them as he had lived there. They disputed the arrangement but, as they couldn't reach an agreement, the Plymstock monks hatched a plan to intercept the body on its way to Tavistock. The bridge over the River Tavy seemed like the perfect place. However, the monks from Tavistock heard of the plan and quickly built another bridge over the Tavy so they could take another route. The monks of Plymstock were fooled, hence the second bridge became known as Guilebridge.

The body was buried in Tavistock Abbey Church, so the spot on the moors is probably where his body was found.

TWO BRIDGES

In the centre of the moors, where the Cowsic and the West Dart converge and the two main roads across Dartmoor cross, is Two Bridges. It is a well-known spot due to the Two Bridges Hotel, a popular hotel and restaurant with gardens running down to the river. It was originally built in the 1780s by Mr Justice Buller, as a pub called the Saracens Head.

Mr Justice Buller was the youngest High Court Judge ever to sit in the British courts. He was thirty-two years of age. In 1787, he built and lived in what is now known as the Prince Hall Hotel, then known as Prynses Hall, further down the road from the Two Bridges Hotel. There was a building here from 1443 and the original foundations and cellars are still under the floors of the present building. It isn't known how the first building was destroyed.

Mr Buller married a local heiress at seventeen and settled down to spend her money. This is when he built the Saracens Head (Two Bridges Hotel). He also made his living room available as a place of worship for the surrounding inhabitants, as there was no church until one was built in Princetown in 1810.

In 1800, Mr Buller died and the Gullet family, who owned the farmstead next door, bought the mansion. They attempted to farm the 2,600 acres of land they now owned but were unsuccessful. The farm changed hands a couple of times and, at one time, the Barringtons, stewards to the Duke of Cornwall, lived here.

Two Bridges Hotel. (Author's collection)

Wistman's Wood

STUNTED OAK

The old man in his wrinkled overcoat
Can no longer have sons;
Those he has fathered are dead
Or almost as old as himself.
Each year frost cracks his skin,
Brittles his bones,
Snaps off another finger;
Birds dance on his shoulders,
Whistle in his ear,
Roost in his hat,
And when they get tired of his company
Fly away, without him.

Fenella Montgomery

This wonderland of moss-covered boulders and gnarled trees covered in lichen is ancient, one of the original wooded areas of Dartmoor. It is one of the most famous woodlands in Britain, known for its stunted oak trees and its thick luxuriant mosses and lichens.

The oaks are pedunculate oak (*see* p.86), which aren't common to Dartmoor. It is the sessile oak that is normally found here. There are over forty-seven different species of mosses and liverworts in these woods, and 119 species of lichen have been recorded here. The wood is a short walk from Two Bridges and well worth it, although it is nearly impossible to enter due to the floor being covered in huge boulders.

Supposedly, it is the most haunted place on Dartmoor and locals won't go near it once the sun begins to set. There is an abundance of legends, tales and ghost stories attached to Wistman's Wood. Legend has it that it was a sacred place for the Druids, and there is a boulder there known as the 'Druids Stone', or the 'Buller Stone', where ceremonies took place.

The wood is also thought to be the home of the Wisht Hounds, the huge black demon dogs with fire in their eyes and hunger for blood in their veins that Dewer (otherwise known as Satan) hunted with (*see* p.81). Other creepy creatures supposed to live here are the hosts of adders, which writhe and wriggle around the boulders and roots, and have more venomous bites than any other adders on Dartmoor. So be careful where you tread!

The lychway (the Way of the Dead) runs nearby, and many people have reported seeing a ghostly procession of men walking slowly through the woods at night.

How Old is Wistman's Wood?

Before 10000 BC, Dartmoor was covered in woodland. The woodland grew up as the climate warmed since the last ice age, and seeds came over from Europe. The land masses were then connected and much of the European vegetation took hold here. When man first arrived on Dartmoor he started to clear the woodlands and eventually, due to this, natural fires, and the formation of peat bogs, Dartmoor lost most of its woodland covering, becoming what it is today.

Why was Wistman's Wood Untouched?

It is surrounded by Bronze Age remains and the rest of the land was obviously cleared. Perhaps it was because it grew out of an area covered with large granite boulders, preventing man from chopping the trees and meaning that not many animals could graze here.

'Wistman's Wood.' (Mike Bartholomew)

Wood Warbler (*Phylloscopus sibilatrix*)

These little birds live in the oak woodlands, hidden by the leaves, flitting about in the treetops hunting insects. They have a yellow-green back and bright yellow breast, and will sometimes sing.

Their nests are built on the ground out of grass, leaves and bracken, and aren't usually very well concealed with their domed roof and sides.

At the end of August/beginning of September, they migrate to the warmer climates of Africa, returning late in April to breed.

Sessile Oak (*Quercus petraea*)

Also native to Europe and the UK, this oak is slightly different to the English oak in that the trunk is longer, the leaves have stems and the acorns do not have stems. The tallest of these trees reach 130ft (40m) high with a fan-shaped crown.

As with the English oak, this tree was a valuable crop and, by the seventeenth century, large areas of the countryside had been denuded of the sessile oak. The wood was used to feed the furnaces of iron smelters, as it burnt steadily and gave off a lot of heat.

Oak bark was once used as a source of tannin for making leather from hides. The hide was softened in a lime pit and all the hairs and flesh were removed, then it was passed through a bath of pounded oak bark and water.

Wood Ant (*Formica rufa*)

Living in the dry woodlands of Dartmoor, this ant is very social and builds its nests in groups to form a community. The nests have a dome of leaves and twigs over them and you can sometimes recognise them on the woodland floor. The ants within a community are friendly towards each other and have a defined territory for hunting, which they guard against hunters from other colonies. When they hunt for food they form a trail. Insects and caterpillars are their main diet. If they are threatened or sat on, they squirt formic acid at the enemy; they can also give a painful nip.

The Powder Mills

On the road from Two Bridges to Postbridge you can see the ruins of old chimneys in the distance. This is the site of the old gunpowder mills and is now a Grade II listed building.

Although a seemingly strange thing to find in the middle of Dartmoor, this was actually the ideal place to set up a gunpowder factory – in a remote place far away from residential areas, close to running water and surrounded by customers. Gunpowder was used by the miners, the farmers and the granite quarries. The mill was built in 1846 by George Frean, who established the Plymouth & Dartmoor Gunpowder Co. The mill used the water from the Cherry Brook and several leats were built from the East Dart River to feed the waterwheels.

How was the Gunpowder Made?

Gunpowder is made from a mixture of sulphur (from volcanic areas of Italy), ground saltpetre (imported from India) and charcoal (from local burners). The ingredients were ground separately in the mills and then specific quantities were mixed (75% saltpetre, 10% sulphur and 15% charcoal). This was crushed, mixed and churned into a crude black powder and then compressed into slabs.

The slabs were broken into granules and sieved; this process was called corning. These corned grains were then tumbled with black lead to give them a coating; this was known as dusting and made the gunpowder waterproof. It was then dried in trays in a furnace, the tall chimneys drawing away the sparks and the fumes. The powder was packed into oak barrels, which were covered in leather to prevent leakage, and was transported by horse and cart to the various storage centres at Ashburton, Newton Abbot, Exeter and Plymouth.

To check the gunpowder was working, a 'proving mortar' (like a small cannon) was used. You can see one by the entrance to the pottery. This would fire a 68lb shot over a measured distance.

In its prime, the mill employed over 100 people: gunpowder makers, blacksmiths, coopers (to make the barrels), carpenters and wheelwrights. They came from all over the moors. When George Frean retired in 1884, a Mr G. Williams took over, but soon the site fell into decline.

Surprisingly, there were few accidents in the factory. Story has it that the workers were made to sit on one-legged stools, so that if they lost concentration or fell asleep they would crash to the floor and be woken with a start before anything more dangerous could happen.

The Powder Mills Pottery

Next door to the ruined gunpowder factory is a working pottery with a gallery full of inspiring work to look around. Joss Hibbs, who lives here with her family, makes all her pottery completely out of the natural material on Dartmoor. The clay comes from the local clayworks and

'Hairy Hands Bridge.' (Miles Wolstenholme)

quarries, the glaze is made from gravel from the river-beds, and the kiln is built out of granite from the moors and fired using wood from the moors. So, if you wish to take a real piece of Dartmoor home with you, this is the place to come.

The Hairy Hands

Travelling along the road from Two Bridges to Postbridge you will cross a bridge, just before the entrance to the Powder Mills Pottery. This bridge looks standard and there is nothing really remarkable about it. However, this is the area where many unexplained road accidents have taken place since the early 1900s. Drivers and cyclists have swerved violently off the road for no apparent reason, most of them reporting that a pair of severed hands grabbed the steering wheel or handle bars and forced them off the edge of the road. Nobody was killed until June 1921, when a medical officer from Dartmoor Prison lost control of his motorbike and died. His children, travelling in the sidecar, survived. A few weeks later, a captain from the army reported that a pair of hairy hands had forced his motorbike off the road too.

In 1924, a lady staying in a caravan on the moors with her husband, near the Powder Mills, reported that she saw a hairy, severed hand trying to get into her caravan at night. She was terrified and made the sign of a cross in front of her – apparently the hand then disappeared.

Some say it is the way the road was built that caused these accidents, but nobody can explain the hands. So beware.

Purple Moor Grass (*Molinia caerulea*)

As its name suggests, moor grass grows on the moors, covering large areas of the marshland. It is the tall straight strong tussocks of grass you see whenever there is wet boggy land ahead. The grass flowers from July to September and the small florets are, of course, purple.

POSTBRIDGE

On the main road between Moretonhampstead and Two Bridges lies Postbridge, a small hamlet with a few houses, a pub, a hotel, an Information Centre and a wonderful shop and post office. Postbridge is known for its clapper bridge, around which it developed. It was built in the thirteenth century to enable packhorses to cross the river on their way to Tavistock, the nearest stannary town. The bridge is still complete, but nowadays the modern road and bridge next to it carries the traffic.

Postbridge is a beautiful place to visit and the clapper bridge is the biggest on Dartmoor so attracts lots of visitors. There is a large car park here with a Dartmoor Information Centre. The local shop and post office is extremely welcoming, providing ice creams, teas, books, and souvenirs.

Dartmoor Bridges

On a moor which is covered with boggy mires, gurgling streams and gushing rivers, there has always been a need for bridges. Before bridges, the simplest way to cross a river was to find its shallowest point and cross there. This was a ford. Where the water was slightly deeper, stepping stones were used and there are many examples of stepping stones on Dartmoor.

Clam Bridges

Where the water was deeper, narrow bridges were created: a tree trunk placed from bank to bank. These wooden bridges were known as clam bridges and there are still a few on Dartmoor. The Mary Tavy Clam is a good example.

Clapper Bridges

Where the river was slightly wider, clapper bridges were built. These were made of huge slabs of granite, being supported on columns of granite slabs or, where the river was narrower, the granite slab would be placed from riverbank to riverbank. Postbridge is a wonderful example, with others at Dartmeet (partially collapsed) and Bellever (also collapsed). There are other clapper bridges dotted around the moors, of various designs, which you might spot.

The word 'clapper' apparently derives from the Saxon or Old English word for 'cleaca', which means 'bridging the stepping stones'.

St Gabriel's Church

As you leave Postbridge, heading for Moretonhampstead, you will see St Gabriel's Church. It was built in 1868 as a mission chapel and became a church in 1934. It is particularly pretty.

The Grey Wagtail (*Motacilla cinerea*)

The rushing, tumbling rivers and streams of Dartmoor are the perfect home for this grey, black and yellow bird, as it can perch on the boulders with its tail bobbing, waiting for an unsuspecting fly or midge to pass its way. Small dragonflies, mayflies and water beetles are also its favourites. Grey wagtails nest in the hollows of tree roots along the riverbanks, or on the ledge of a stone wall or bridge.

Roe Deer (*Capreolus capreolus*)

The UK's native deer, the roe deer, has lived in Britain since at least 400,000 years ago. The species was thriving until 1338, when it was declared that roe deer wasn't good enough to be hunted by noblemen, and soon became game for the starving peasants. By the late 1500s they were extinct in Wales and gone from large areas of England and Scotland. However, the forestry boom in the eighteenth and nineteenth centuries, along with the increase in hunting, brought them back.

On Dartmoor you may see one of these magnificent, gentle animals wandering amidst the trees of the woodlands.

'Bellever Clapper.' (Miles Wolstenholme)

'Postbridge Clapper.' (Miles Wolstenholme)

'Grey Wagtail.' (Miles Wolstenholme)

'Burial Chamber in Bellever Forest.' (Miles Wolstenholme)

BELLEVER

About 2km (1 mile) south of Postbridge is a small hamlet, a cluster of houses near the East Dart River, known as Bellever. The first record of settlement here is in a Duchy of Cornwall record dated 1355. The name of the farm was Welford (contraction of 'wielle', meaning spring and ford) and it consisted of a farmhouse, outbuildings and workers' cottages. It was owned by the Duchy of Cornwall.

In 1930, the farm was sold to the Forestry Commission and, in 1934, a few of the barns were let to the Youth Hostels Association and turned into a hostel. There is still a youth hostel there today, the oldest in Devon.

The Forestry Commission began a large planting scheme in 1921 and, in the 1950s, several houses were built here to house the workers. The forest was being planted to replenish wood supplies, but unfortunately the trees were planted right on top of an area covered with prehistoric remains.

Lakehead Hill

At Lakehead Hill, now a clearing of the forest plantation, you can see a settlement enclosure with several hut circles inside the wall and one outside. This is known as Kraps Ring. It is thought that the enclosure wall would have been about 2m thick and 1m high. During excavation in 1895, one hut was discovered, still intact, with a cooking hole and a hearth for the fire.

Nearby are several Bronze Age stone circles, rows and cairns; many of them were looted years ago in the search for treasure, and many stones were removed to build walls. The area was clearly of ritual and spiritual importance.

There are numerous prehistoric sites here which were covered by the Forestry Commission, but the area is now slowly being cleared to reveal many of these features.

Bellever Tor

South of Kraps Ring stands Bellever Tor, and on its slopes is a prehistoric burial complex with around ten cairns. On the slopes of the tor are the remains of several field systems and a couple of enclosures. On the north-west slope is what is classified as a 'rock shelter', which dates to prehistoric times. It is a shelter, 10ft by 4ft, built between two large boulders – the back end blocked by a stone wall. Inside, a cooking hole was found along with around sixty-six worked flints.

Despite the signs of this being a settlement area, there are no signs of any stone rows or circles here. It was obviously not a sacred spot for prehistoric man.

Today, there is a large car park at Bellever and, during the summer, the grassy area by the River Dart is packed. It is a popular tourist spot, with the shallow winding river being ideal for children to paddle in and the flat grassy banks ideal for picnics and barbecues, all within easy reach of the car.

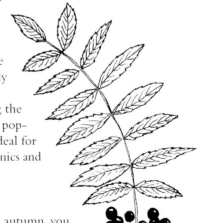

Rowan or Mountain Ash (*Sorbus aucuparia*)

When the branches of this tree are laden with berries in autumn, you can understand why the rowan was given its name. Supposedly, 'rowan' derives from the Norse word 'runa', which means 'a charm'.

The rowan grows well beside the rushing Dartmoor streams and, as its alternative name implies, it thrives best on high ground and mountain sides, often sprouting from between two boulders where its seed was dropped by a bird.

In ancient times, the tree was planted outside houses and in churchyards to ward off witches. Sometimes its branches were hung in the house to conserve the quality of water. The red berries can be made into a jelly, which is eaten with game. They are rich in vitamin C and were once made into a drink to prevent scurvy.

The wood of the rowan is strong and flexible, and yellow–grey in colour. It has been used to make tool handles and small, carved objects.

The Warren House Inn

Standing alone in the centre of the moors, looking out towards Hookney Tor and Soussons Down, is the wonderfully atmospheric Warren House Inn. Easy to find by the side of the main B3212 from Moretonhampstead, this pub is a great place to stop and eat. On a warm summer's day you can sit outside on the benches on the moorland opposite or, if it's chilly, you can cosy up inside and watch the fire, which has apparently never gone out.

This pub is reportedly the third highest in England and probably the loneliest. The existing inn was built in 1845 for the miners from the Vitifer, Birch Tor and Golden Dagger mines below. These were flourishing during the 1800s. The original inn here, though, was built on the opposite side of the road and was called the New House. It is assumed that the name was changed to reflect the surrounding rabbit warrens. The sign above the door, of three rabbits or hares chasing each other, is known as a tinners' rabbit and is found on many roof bosses in churches throughout Dartmoor.

According to Dartmoor folklore, the peat fire in the pub was 'always in' and, when the new inn was finished, the landlord carried the burning peat (vags) over to the new fireplace where he stoked it up; apparently it has never gone out since then, though wood is now burnt rather than vags.

The Inn Today

Today the inn is busy and still atmospheric, and the fire always burns whatever the weather. As is the case with much of the surrounding area, the inn is owned by the Duchy of Cornwall. It is run as a freehold and is totally self sufficient with no mains supplies.

'The Warren House Inn.' (Miles Wolstenholme)

Salted Down Feyther

Legend goes that, years ago, an unknown traveller was making his way across the moors when he was caught out by a sudden change in the weather. The mist swirled down, damp and thick, causing him to lose his way – and then the rain came, pouring relentlessly until it was dark. The poor traveller was stumbling along, completely lost, when he spotted a light glowing in the distance. He headed towards it and soon discovered the Warren House Inn.

Extremely relieved, he banged on the door as it was already closed for the night. The innkeeper answered and the traveller asked for a room for the night. Unfortunately there were none free but, with further pleading from the miserable, wet traveller, the innkeeper gave in, 'We've got a room with salted down feyther in, if you don't mind that.' The traveller accepted quickly and was soon tucked up in a warm bed.

The next morning he awoke refreshed, and happy to see the sun shining through the window. He dressed and packed, and was just leaving the room when he remembered what the innkeeper had said about a 'salted down feyther'. Curious to know what it was, he looked around. All he could see was a large chest at the foot of the bed. He opened it to peer inside and, to his shock, discovered a dead man inside wrapped in white cloths. Horrified, he rushed downstairs to escape this strange place – only to find the innkeeper and his family enjoying breakfast together. On being invited to join them, the traveller accepted and sat down. He told them what he had seen and they laughed out loud.

'I thought you said you didn't mind being in a room with salted down feyther,' exclaimed the innkeeper, and went on to explain that his wife's father had passed away a couple of weeks ago and, because of the bad weather, they hadn't been able to take him to Lydford for burial and so had salted him down to preserve his body.

The traveller smiled to himself and realised the he had misunderstood the innkeeper's local dialect. He had actually meant 'salted down father'.

The Birch Tor, Vitifer and Golden Dagger Tin Mines

A short walk down from the Warren House Inn, heading south, is what is now a pretty, flat grassy area amongst the surrounding rough, heather-covered moorland. A clear trickling stream wanders through the dip and a couple of gnarled trees grow beside the remains of old stone buildings – evidence of the past tin mining activity that took place here.

Birch Tor Mine and the Vitifer Mine were opened in 1852 by the New Birch Tor and Vitifers Consols Tin Mining Co. In 1866, the mines were producing 95 tons of black tin and employed 120 people. They were the most productive mines on Dartmoor. The miners who worked here were cast-offs from other mining companies, who had left because they had committed minor offences. Work in the mines was tough and conditions were hard. The accommodation was terrible, and at one stage the miners were sharing beds; as one got out of bed to work another took his place to sleep. By 1886, the mine was abandoned and although a new lease was obtained and part of the mine was reopened, by the beginning of the war they were completely closed.

Close by are the remains of a stone building known as Dinah's House. It is thought that this was a meeting place for the miners. You can also see the remains of the mine workings, the engine house and a miners' dry.

Hawthorn (*Crataegus monogyna*)

Hawthorn will crop up nearly anywhere and is fast growing and sturdy. It has been used for centuries as field boundaries, the dense foliage and sharp thorns growing rapidly to form a solid barrier.

'Vitifer Tin Mine.' (Miles Wolstenholme)

'Dinah's House at Golden Dagger.' (Miles Wolstenholme)

'Hawthorn at Coombestone Tor.' (Mike Bartholomew)

The fleshy fruits of the hawthorn, called haws, turn full and dark red in the autumn and provide food for many birds. They are rich in vitamin C and can be made into a jelly for human consumption too.

On Dartmoor you will see an occasional solitary, windswept hawthorn, shaped by the direction of the wind but still growing, a stunning reminder of the wildness of the environment.

The hawthorn is also known as the may tree or quickthorn, and in the countryside it is believed that if you destroy a hawthorn, peril will come upon you and if you bring the spring blossom into your home you are inviting in disaster.

GRIMSPOUND

This is one of the most well known and loved prehistoric archaeological sites on Dartmoor. A wonderful Bronze Age settlement, just a short walk up the hill from the road. Here you can clearly see the remains of an enclosure wall and the hut circle within it. Its location is high and the views are worth the little climb.

Grimspound is around 4 acres in size and is a settlement of twenty-four huts, enclosed within what was once a very thick and strong stone wall. It is thought that the settlement wasn't a defensive settlement but a pound, hence its name, and the wall is apparently the thickest and strongest pound wall on Dartmoor

The remains of the huts are still there. Some of them weren't dwellings but rather used as storage places or animal pens. The ones that were lived in had hearths and cooking holes inside. It appears that prehistoric man heated his water by heating stones on the fire and then dropping them in the pot of water. Their clay pots weren't fireproof then. Next to the doorways were the beds, built from granite slabs, covered with heather and then animal skins.

Excavations have shown that the enclosure wall around the huts was actually two separate walls, one inside the other, about 3.7m wide and 1.7m high. The walls were built of granite and had supporting cross beams between them, also made of granite. The original entrance to the pound is clearly visible as you approach from the road, and you can see two other entrances on the other sides which were built in the thirteenth and fourteenth centuries by miners. The track linked the Manaton and West Webburn tin mines and was known as the Miners Path.

The Skylark (*Alauda arvensis*)

On a warm summer's day on the open moor, high above and usually hard to spot, you can often hear the clear and constant warbling of a skylark. It will rise several hundred feet vertically and hover, singing for a few minutes, then sink down until it touches the ground. They nest in hollows on the ground or concealed in a clump of long grass.

CHALLACOMBE

All around the area you can see evidence that people settled in Challacombe during the Bronze Age, but the first written evidence of people here is in the Domesday Book, in which Challacombe Manor was recorded.

Close to Challacombe Farmhouse you can see the remains of around seven medieval houses, one of them once being a Dartmoor longhouse.

In 1505 it was recorded that a 'vill', a small hamlet, called Chalnecombe existed here and the people living here were considered special tenants of the king. This meant that they could take what they liked from the land, except for oak and venison. They could gather stone, cut peat and graze cattle, in return for a small rent and helping with the annual cattle and pony drifts (*see* p.22).

By 1613 there were five tenements at Challacombe, which were in use until 1880. It seems that one of the buildings became a cider house, designed to serve the miners from the nearby tin mines. Most of the inhabitants here would have made a living from farming and mining.

There is a tall stone wall encircling acres of the land, evidence of warrening or rabbit farming (*see* p.85). Headland Warren, which gives its name to the adjoining farm, was established around 1700. The warren enclosures are known locally as the 'playing card fields' and here you can see a number of 'pillow mounds' or artificial burrows. The rabbit meat must have helped feed the mining population.

Heath Milkwort (*Polygala serpyllifolia*)

Growing on the heaths, this plant normally has blue flowers but can be pink or purple. An infusion of milkwort has been known to increase the flow of a nursing mother's milk; it was also used for chesty coughs and to purify the blood.

Adder (*Vipera berus*)

Also known as the viper, the adder is Britain's only poisonous snake – but it isn't a threat to a healthy adult. Its bite does not always release venom, but when it does it can cause painful swelling, sickness and fever, and an anti-venom treatment from hospital is needed.

Adders live in some grassy stone banks on the moorland heath. They are about 50-60cm long, with a distinctive dark zigzag pattern running down the length of the back and a dark V-shaped mark on the head.

'Hut Circle at Grimspound.' (Miles Wolstenholme)

'Challacombe Medieval Village.' (Miles Wolstenholme)

'Challacombe Stone Row.' (Miles Wolstenholme)

If you spot an adder it will slink away from you; it is illegal to harm or kill a UK snake, so don't hit it with a stick!

Adders' eggs hatch inside the female and the young are born alive rather than in their eggs.

DARTMEET

As the name suggests, Dartmeet is where the East Dart and the West Dart meet to form the River Dart. The road bridge was built in 1792 and crosses the East Dart. Next to it are the remains of an ancient clapper bridge, dating back to medieval times. The old clapper bridge was washed away in 1826 but was rebuilt in 1888. It appears to have been washed away again, as it is now partially collapsed.

The two rivers meet just downstream of the bridges, flowing onward to Buckfast and ultimately to the river's end at Dartmouth.

Dartmeet has become a well-known tourist attraction, with people coming here to experience the rush of the rivers, the Dartmoor woods and the open moor. There is now a large car park here; during the summer it is crammed and the riverbanks are filled with the brightly coloured paraphernalia of tourists.

Further up the West Dart you will find Pixies Wood. It is here that the Dartmoor pixies are supposed to live, in small tunnels underneath the sycamore trees. Up the hill from the bridge, by the side of the road, you will find 'Pixieland' – where you can buy your own Dartmoor pixie and take him home. Pixies Holt is a nearby outdoor education centre.

You might start to believe that pixies really do live here. There is a story of pixies in the area; it starts at what is now the Badgers Holt tearoom in the car park, which declares itself to be 'the most famous tearoom on the moor'. This tearoom was once two cottages, Joe Leaman lived in one...

'Dartmoor Tree.' (Mike Bartholomew)

Joe Leaman and the Piskies

Joe Leaman had lived and worked on Dartmoor all his life. He was retired and enjoying life in his cottage down where the rivers meet. Familiar with the ways of the moor, he always remembered what his mother said. 'Joe,' she would say, 'never mind what 'ee does in life, don't 'ee be upsetting the piskies. No gurd will come of it, it won't.'

One cold winter's day, Joe went off to Brimpts Plantation to cut some wood for his fire. He enjoyed himself, chopping the sticks, which he tied together and carried to the edge of the plantation. He then returned to cut some more, pushing his walking stick into the ground next to his bundle so he could find it again.

Unbeknown to Joe, a group of young local lads were watching him from behind some bushes and decided they would have some fun. When he was gone, they picked up his bundle of sticks and hid it.

A little while later, Joe carried his second bundle happily back to the edge of the plantation. He stopped and looked around, frowning when he saw that his first bundle had gone. He looked around and then laid the second bundle where he had left the first. This time he stuck his walking stick right through the bundle, thinking this might stop it disappearing so easily, and off he walked back into the woods to chop some more.

Of course, the young lads dashed out from behind their bush, chuckling, and removed the second bundle, putting Joe's stick back where it had been in the ground. When Joe returned with his third load of sticks he just stared at the place where he had left his bundles. Then he dropped his third bundle of wood and walked off quickly back to his cottage, feeling very ill at ease. As it was evening, he decided to cook his dinner and have an early night.

The young lads laughed as they watched poor Joe rushing home, but they decided to play one last prank on him. That night they carried the three bundles of sticks down from the plantation and left them outside Joe's front door.

'Grey Squirrel.' (Mike Bartholomew)

When the morning came, Joe got up as usual and ate his breakfast, still feeling uneasy about what had happened the evening before. He washed up and, as he opened the front door to go outside, he saw his three bundles of wood lying right in front of him. His face lit up with relief. He said to himself, 'Ah. Those piskies must be friends wiv 'ee again. It would ne'er do to go upsetting them piskies.'

The Dipper (*Cinclus cinclus*)

You can often see dippers perched on a boulder in a stream. A dipper is a wren-like bird with a dark brown top half and white throat and breast; it will be constantly bobbing its tail. This little bird actually finds its food at the bottom of the stream. It dives down into the water and walks along the bottom with its head down against the current, searching for water insects, tadpoles and worms. Dippers can swim on or under the water, and they will often spend a whole year on the same stretch. They nest under bridges, or under the overhang of a riverbank in a domed nest built of moss. Baby dippers can swim before they can fly.

Grey Squirrel (*Sciurus carolinensis*)

The grey squirrel was introduced to the UK from North America at the end of the nineteenth century and has now taken the place of the native red squirrel. Common around the woodlands of Dartmoor, the grey squirrel is considered a pest and is hated by bird lovers as it raids birds' nests for eggs and chicks.

Its favourite foods are hazelnuts and acorns, and it buries them in the ground for the winter months. It builds its nest, called a drey, in tree branches and has two litters per year of up to seven babies.

Coombestone Tor

Right by the side of the road from Dartmeet to Holne is Coombestone Tor. There is a car park right in front of the tor so, for those who prefer not to walk too far, this is the perfect way to see some fine examples of Dartmoor geology. This tor clearly shows the effects of erosion and jointing (*see* p.9), which is the process by which tors are formed. On its summit are some good examples of rock basins (*see* p.12). There are also some beautiful views over the moors from here.

PHOTOGRAPHY

MIKE BARTHOLOMEW

I am a landscape and nature photographer who has lived in Devon all of my life. My interest in Dartmoor started when I was a child, with memories of picnics by the rivers, flying kites on windy hills and seeing the Dartmoor ponies. Whilst at school I gained different memories of Dartmoor, as I discovered the rapidly changing weather and often harsh conditions while taking part in the Ten-Tors challenge training. It wasn't until later, after discovering photography, that I set out to capture the spirit of Dartmoor and explore more of this landscape that draws people back time after time.

I spend most of my time on Dartmoor at either sunrise or sunset, as these produce the most magical lighting conditions. I don't think I'll ever tire of Dartmoor as a photographic subject, as you'll never see the same thing twice. It never ceases to amaze me how the landscape changes so dramatically throughout the seasons, from its snow-covered rolling hills in the winter, to its meadows bursting with bluebells in the spring.
www.mikebartholomew.com

MILES WOLSTENHOLME

I am a keen rambler and outdoor photographer living in West Devon. When not working from home as a web developer, I relish the opportunity to escape into the surrounding countryside with my camera and a flask of coffee. With the northern flank of Dartmoor National Park just minutes from my front door, I can often be found walking the East Okement Valley to Belstone and the adjacent northern moor.

Photography has always been a passion of mine, especially when coupled with my love of the West Country. It provides a very welcome opportunity for both fresh air and quiet contemplation, away from the office and everyday distractions. Looking through the lens forces me to look at everything with a fresh pair of eyes, to re-evaluate the world before me. It's like being a child all over again – but with much more expensive toys!
www.dartmoorandbeyond.co.uk

BIBLIOGRAPHY

Crossing, William, *Crossing's Guide to Dartmoor*, 1912 edition, David & Charles

Gant, T.H. and Copley, W.L., *Dartmoor Legends Retold*, Baron Jay Ltd, 1990

Gant, T.H. and Copley, W.L., *More Dartmoor Legends and Customs*, Baron Jay Ltd

Keble Martin, W., *The Concise British Flora in Colour*, George Rainbird Ltd, 1965

Reader's Digest Field Guide to Birds of Britain, 1981

Reader's Digest Field Guide to the Trees and Shrubs of Britain, 1981

Thurlow, George, *Thurlow's Dartmoor Companion*, Peninsula Press, 2001

There are many history groups on Dartmoor, and many of the parishes have websites and village books full of information to which I have referred. You will find more details of each parish on their websites.

www.legendarydartmoor.co.uk: Legendary Dartmoor by Tim Sandles. This website is crammed with information for those wishing to find out more about the ancient sites and legends.

www.dartmoor-npa.gov.uk: Dartmoor National Park Authority website, which provides information and educational material on all aspects of the moors.

www.dartmoor-crosses.org: A guide to Dartmoor crosses.

INDEX

Printed in Great Britain
by Amazon